Cooperative Lobbying— The Power of Pressure

Cooperative Lobbying – The Power of Pressure

DONALD R. HALL

Illustrated by George Fisher

THE UNIVERSITY OF ARIZONA PRESS

Tucson, Arizona

About the Author...

DONALD R. HALL unfolds his interpretation from
the vantage point of a professor of government
and research specialist in the Institute of Government Research at the University of Arizona. Earlier
he taught in the department of political science at
the University of Colorado and was a guest scholar
at Brookings Institution in 1965. Active in political
affairs in his former home town of Little Rock,
Arkansas, Dr. Hall has authored a number of publications concerning elections and practical politics.
He holds a B.A. from the University of Chicago
and an M.A. and a Ph.D. from the University of
Colorado.

THE UNIVERSITY OF ARIZONA PRESS

Contents

ing terms and of lumping their opposition together under the worst label they can find. I have been surprised over the high quality of business lobbyists that I have met in Washington." [18]

An example of the prejudice felt by some groups toward lobbyists working for opposing groups is evidenced in the paragraphs following, quoted from a leaflet distributed at an AFL-CIO legislative strategy meeting in 1965, during the controversy over passage of H.R. 77, the right-to-work bill:

A new, more sophisticated breed of demagogue has taken over the leadership of the extreme right in the United States and nowhere is this more evident than in the smoothly professional campaign to outlaw the union shop through "right to work" laws.

The cross-burners and the panting, shirtsleeved apostles of hate, fear and prejudice have not disappeared from the American scene. But they have been largely relegated to the side show, while the center ring is taken over by well-groomed businessmen high in the ranks of the U.S. Chamber of Commerce and the National Association of Manufacturers — and, in many cases, luminaries of the John Birch Society as well . . . .

Like the Communists, whose tactics they emulate, the Birchers and other cadres of the radical right find it effective to conceal their true aims behind the masks of high-sounding slogans and "front" organizations . . . .[19]

Another aspect of lobbying as a profession, a disadvantage it shares with other forms of corporate activity, is that the lobbyist is often subjected to guerrilla warfare within his own organization. He may get caught in the intricacies of intragroup politics; he may find himself trapped between majority and minority interests in his organization; or he may find that he has a personality conflict with his organization's staff director. Since both lobbyists and the paid "executive directors" or managers of large associations tend to be extroverts and to relish recognition, a basis for personal conflict exists in many groups. As one lobbyist said, in reference to the national Chamber of Commerce and its paid executive vice president, "There's room for only one star in that show."

Relations with the group's membership is also a problem for some lobbyists. Said one: "You have to get along with the members. But sometimes it isn't easy. The big shots, the company presidents, will treat

---

[18] Interview with Paul Wagner, Washington, D. C., July 26, 1965.

[19] David L. Perlman, "The New Breed of Demagogue." Mr. Perlman is an assistant editor of the *AFL-CIO News*.

you like a hired hand, when it's their necks you're saving; and the little guys from Podunk — who are too ignorant to understand what lobbying is all about — look down on you for doing it."

But the most consistent disadvantage, according to many lobbyists, is that so much time must be consumed in explaining to members what their own interests *really* are and how they are being jeopardized. Lobbyists, however, tend to overstate difficulties involved in arousing the membership, and to overstate the intensity and relative importance of a crisis, as many readily admit. This aura of crisis is often described as "necessary to keep the membership aroused." What the lobbyist objects to most strenuously is the necessity to plead for support when he feels the need for support is obvious and inescapable. He *knows,* for example, that the X Bill can be beaten if Congressman Y receives personal telephone calls from ten respected constituents opposing the bill. But the lobbyist may have to contact fifty or more key people from the Congressman's district before he can muster the needed phone calls. The others contacted, whose interests also are at stake, are "too busy," "not interested in this bill at this time," or "don't want to get involved."

The occasionally tense relationship between the lobbyist (or staff member) and the membership at large has been cited as a reason for the mutual disenchantment sometimes existing between trade association men and their members. Bauer, Pool, and Dexter stress this disenchantment, saying that the most successful roles of the trade association executive are as arbitrator among conflicting forces within his own group and as spokesman for whatever policies result from this conflict. In addition, the executive serves as a "go-between" who keeps lines of contact open among members and among persons outside the organization on whom the executive depends when he wants something done.[20]

All this leads one to expect that polling association members would establish that the membership does not think too highly of its executives and lobbyists. Such is not the case. A survey of all associations affiliated with the national Chamber of Commerce asked members to rate the performances of their associations and executives. Tabulation of answers to several questions [21] indicates a generally high degree of

---

[20] Raymond A. Bauer, Ithiel de Sola Pool, and Lewis Anthony Dexter, *American Business and Public Policy* (New York: Atherton Press, 1964), pp. 330-31; © 1963, by permission of Publishers, Atherton Press, all rights reserved.

[21] "A Study of the Views of Members and Association Executives," prepared by Opinion Research Corporation, Princeton, New Jersey, for the Chamber of Commerce of the United States, 1965-66. Questions and answers quoted above are from the preliminary report of the results and should not be held to be necessarily final. Survey made available to the author through the courtesy of the national Chamber.

satisfaction with performances and accomplishments of associations and their staffs:

(a) Say association does *good* job on . . .

	Businessmen	Professional Men
Government relations	84%	64%
Statistical information	77%	65%
P.R. and publicity	75%	56%
Education and training	74%	71%

(b) Effectiveness of lobbying and legislative activities?

	Businessmen	Professional Men
Good	67%	50%

(c) Rating of top executive staff member on performance:

	Excellent	Good
All members	45%	34%
Associations with membership:		
Less than 200	66%	23%
200-499	63%	18%
500-9,999	45%	37%
10,000 or more	33%	41%

In summary, lobbying offers good pay and security, wide social contacts, a feeling of "being on the inside" in major decisions. Disadvantages for the lobbyist include considerable subservience to the group and its purposes — and often to men of a caliber the lobbyist regards as inferior to himself. The lobbyist must be able to adjust to living with the "bad public image" of his profession. He is often subjected to conflicts within his own organization; and he often feels that too much of his work necessitates explaining the obvious to members who appear to have little motivation to assist him in protecting their interests.

Training the Organization's Lobbyists

Training given association executives and lobbyists varies in thoroughness according to whether or not the person is expected to carry out intergroup assignments. Intergroup lobbying, in which groups try to form alliances and/or cement good relations with other groups, demands a greater expertise than the formal and informal training given the staff or non-intergroup lobbyist; for the intergroup lobbyist will be called upon to impress, educate, entreat and negotiate with *other lobbyists* in addition to governmental officials.

Formal training for association executives and lobbyists occurs at several levels. First, schools of association management are operated by various national organizations. The national Chamber of Commerce annually conducts six "Institutes for Organization Management," each serving a large geographical area. "With a full range of courses in the fundamentals of management, advanced management studies, and an academy course for graduate students, the Institutes have something for everyone who wants to attain a higher level of personal performance within his organization." [22]

Similar training programs are conducted by the American Society of Association Executives and the American Management Association. Joint, or cooperative, seminars are conducted by public relations societies, personnel associations, etc., which are open to all interested organizations. Evening classes and correspondence courses in executive training are offered by many local colleges and universities.

The "informal" training given association personnel usually consists of on-the-job training as assistants in the organization's various departments. Future lobbyists may develop from departmental assistants or managers; occasionally, "field men" serving the association in a non-Washington location may be brought in to be trained and/or deployed as lobbyists at the direction of the Washington office. How an organization utilizes its personnel depends on the particular organization, its budget, its participation in lobbying activities, and upon organizational policy.

A lobbyist for the American Farm Bureau Federation reported that his method for training assistants was to "take 'em with me to the Hill." While this technique might be effective in some instances, most lobbyists agree that personal contacts and friendships between representatives of organizations and members of Congress and its staff could not be passed along from hand to hand or generation to generation.

Much of a lobbyist's informal training results from his own research, his daily contacts, his information exchanges, and personal relationships he develops with staff members and lobbyists of other organizations. These intergroup contacts are the basis for the lobbyist's future intergroup cooperative lobbying. Most of this intergroup contact is informal and unstructured; in one instance, it might amount to no more than a casual tip from another lobbyist: "You can get to Congressman X by way of his personal secretary, but don't try going through his

---

[22] Chamber of Commerce of the United States, *Finding and Applying Private-Business Solutions to National Problems* (Washington, D. C., Chamber of Commerce of the United States, 1964), p. 19.

legislative assistant." Or, "You can't plant industry items in the *Washington Post* now; that new night editor has a hawk eye for fluff."

Briefly, then, the amount of training, formal or informal, that a lobbyist receives seems to be directly proportional to the amount of lobbying he will be expected to do. If his department makes few trips to the Hill, or if he has to do his lobbying through his association's "governmental affairs department," he will undoubtedly receive little training related to lobbying and may have only limited contacts outside the organization. But if the lobbyist is in a department which frequently testifies before congressional committees or federal agencies, or if there is no legislative affairs section in his organization, he must develop himself as a lobbyist, or his employers will ensure that he receives adequate training.

It is important to note that there appears to be no "training program" for *intergroup* lobbyists. Unlike the lobbyist who concentrates directly upon contacts with government, the intergroup lobbyist must informally acquire whatever experience he needs before he will receive an intergroup assignment. He must become "known" and well thought of as personable and competent. In short, his employers (and their actual or potential allies) must judge him "ready" in the same mysterious way an expert chef knows when a soufflé is "done."

ASSIGNING LOBBYISTS TO INTERGROUP WORK

Assignment of Lobbyists From Within the Organization

Whether an organization sends a man to an intergroup meeting or assigns him to an intergroup project depends initially upon the organization's resources, commitments, goals, and policies. Also, assignment of personnel depends upon "who knows whom" in organizations expected to attend an intergroup meeting. Most groups have their own channels of information and access to other groups. These are personal channels between individuals, i.e., A from X organization knows B in Y organization, but D in X organization may have close contacts only with Z in Y organization.

Which particular person is given an intergroup assignment may depend upon the degree to which the organization feels it will be called upon to commit itself. Obviously, an assistant department manager cannot commit the resources or name of the organization as freely as can the head of the legislative affairs department. Similarly, persons with low rank or inadequate experience will not be assigned to intergroup meetings where they will be outranked or "outclassed."

Assignments to intergroup work may depend upon the organization leader's or manager's judgment as to who would be the best agent.

In turn, this decision is sometimes influenced by relations existing between the group leader and his staff. In at least one known case, the logical person to attend an intergroup meeting was not assigned because the organization's leader was jealous of the growing reputation of the department head. On the other hand, another group leader reported that he felt unable to assign a particularly competent person to an intergroup project because "he is too busy trying to set up a good deal for himself — he's only using us as a springboard for a better assignment with another organization."

The primary qualification for intergroup work is that the organization's representative be acceptable to other groups involved. Acceptance will depend upon what the other groups want the representative to contribute to the project: his contacts, skills, ability to win friends, capabilities as an administrator or "follow through" man, or his authority to commit his organization's resources, name, or personnel.

However, the personal element in intergroup lobbying activities can be overemphasized. Some of the most successful organizations have *no* "assignment" policy determining who will be sent to an intergroup meeting or assigned to a cooperative lobbying effort; whoever is available goes.

The Chamber of Commerce of the United States has a general rule that each department does its own lobbying. Yet, in the third quarter of 1965, only William J. Fannin, Don A. Goodall, Eugene A. Keeney, John R. Miles, and Spencer A. Johnson were registered as Chamber lobbyists.[23] Of these five, only Goodall, Miles and Keeney were listed as department managers on the Chamber's staff organizational chart. No lobbyists were listed for the other twelve Chamber departments. Obviously, not every department has a *registered* lobbyist to represent its interests before government bodies.

Legislative affairs of the national Chamber of Commerce are coordinated by the Chamber's Legislative Department, formerly headed by Theron J. (Terry) Rice. According to Deakin's description of this department, "The legislative department comprises 12 persons out of the Chamber's 350 Washington employees, but that does not begin to tell the story. The legislative office is the conduit through which flows the work of the Chamber's other departments on its way to Capitol Hill.

"To illustrate how this complex lobbying juggernaut works, let us suppose that the President has proposed an education program to Congress. The Chamber's education department goes to work on re-

---

[23] *Congressional Record,* January 10, 1966, pp. 45-77.

search. The White House education message is dissected and analyzed. The results are transmitted to the news and legislative departments, to be sent out to the Chamber's businessman members in "Washington Report," "Congressional Action" and other Chamber publications. When the House and Senate education subcommittees hold hearings on the education bill, the legislative department works with the education department in lining up the witnesses who will testify for the Chamber, writing their testimony and briefing them on the questions to expect from the Congressmen." [24]

Nothing appears on the surface of this account to indicate that the Chamber is doing anything other than making skillful use of its staff and its communications capabilities to inform Congress and Chamber members about an issue which may be of vital interest to them. According to Rice, about three-fourths of the Washington office's time is spent in just such research and its publicity. The problem is, the Chamber does not report expenses of this research and publicity as "lobbying expenses," although the research was conducted "in the hope that they [Chamber members] would exert their influence on legislation." [25]

The Chamber's reason for not reporting these expenses is that the Chamber feels the *U.S. vs. Harriss* decision defines the functions and purposes of organizations in such a way that multipurpose organizations (like the Chamber) are not obliged to report under the Lobbying Act. As Deakin reports, "The United States Chamber of Commerce files reports under the Lobbying Act but attaches a disclaimer, stating that 'legal counsel has advised that in the light of the . . . decision in *U.S. vs. Harriss* [347 U.S. 612 (1954)] . . . it does not appear that the functions and purposes of the Chamber . . . are of such character as to require reporting under the Regulation of Lobbying Act.' The Chamber states it is a multipurpose organization, that its 'principal purpose' is not lobbying, that all of its membership dues and other receipts go for the full purposes of the Chamber and that none are earmarked for specific purposes, legislative or otherwise."

In effect, the Chamber reports expenses it feels "might" be subject to the lobbying law, $45,019 in a nine-month period in 1962, according to Deakin, but does not report expenses related to research or activities involved with "grassroots" lobbying—expenses totalling $3,000,000 that same year.[26]

---

[24] Deakin, *op. cit.*, p. 132.
[25] *Ibid.*, p. 23.
[26] *Ibid.*, pp. 247-48.

Whether or not the Chamber follows its own general rule that "each department takes care of its own lobbying," other less compartmentalized organizations tend to follow the "send whoever is free at the moment" rule when assigning personnel to intergroup meetings or projects.

The National Small Business Association, according to one of its spokesmen, had "considerable flexibility" in assignment of personnel: "Which person from our staff goes to a meeting depends primarily on who is free and on the nature of the meeting. On the other hand, the Chamber of Commerce goes strictly by departments and categories. A departmental manager in transportation will go to a meeting which concerns transportation and no one else will go. This is primarily because departmental managers are the people in the Chamber most informed on the subjects that concern their departments. As to what the Chamber departmental manager will do or say, that is determined by what their policy book says about the issue." [27]

The American Bankers Association and the National Consumers League report that assignment of their personnel depends upon the particular issue under consideration and upon whatever staff member is available for the assignment.

If there *is* any significant pattern regarding assignment of personnel to regular and intergroup lobbying, it is this: "departmentalized" organizations, such as the national Chamber and the NAM, tend to register managers of key departments as lobbyists. Those men are then able to lobby the government and to participate in intergroup lobbying. Small associations usually have few personnel; thus, a few staff members often have to do double duty, lobbying both government and other groups. It is exceptional for an organization, if it can afford several lobbyists, to choose to assign only the same one or two representatives to attend all intergroup meetings and perform all government lobbying.

In addition to the standard lobbying groups, there are many "one man shows" in Washington consisting of a telephone answering service and one lobbyist who "carries his office in his hat," has no staff, and yet is often a key leader in important lobbying. Such a "lone wolf" obviously has limited time for intergroup meetings; he has no group or staff to handle pending matters.

Assignment of "Outside" Lobbyists

Few organizations comment on this subject; the most frequently heard remark is to the effect, "we sometimes hire an outside man or two to represent us, if we have urgent need of his particular specialty.

---

[27] Interview with Herbert Liebenson, Washington, D. C., August 19, 1965.

But ordinarily we do our own work." Apart from this general acknowl-
edgment, most groups do not discuss the use of non-organization personnel for either regular lobbying or intergroup assignments. Therefore,
the following paragraphs concerning assignment of outside personnel
are supported by limited evidence.

There seem to be four logical situations which may prompt an
organization to make use of an outside lobbyist.

First, an outside lobbyist may have particular contacts of special
value in certain circumstances. The lobbyist may know the key persons
in another group; he may have a personal relationship with a major
governmental leader involved in the issue, or he may be able to
arrange introductions to such figures.

Second, the outside lobbyist may have special skills required to
ensure a project's success. This reason is most often advanced by
groups admitting occasional use of "outside" personnel. The National
Automobile Dealers Association, for example, has hired outside counsel
upon occasion, for the sole purpose of negotiating certain contracts.
The American Medical Association has made almost continuous use
of the Whitaker and Baxter public relations firm to organize and
manage the AMA's campaign against Medicare. Other groups with
highly qualified lobbyists on their payrolls often retain a public relations or legal firm to manage specific campaigns on major issues or
to provide access to key government personnel. The National Retail
Merchants Association, for example, has employed one of the best
lobbyists in Washington, John Hazen; yet the NRMA also retains
the Arnold, Fortas and Porter law firm, widely known for its influential
contacts among government leaders.

Third, a group may "borrow" the services of another group's
lobbyist for certain tasks, if an intergroup alliance has first been
formed. It is possible that a group without its own lobbyist *might* join
an intergroup alliance solely to make use of the lobbying personnel of
other groups. This parallels the situations of many small interests which
band together in an association to divide, or "pro-rate," the cost of a
single lobbyist among them all.

Fourth, an intergroup alliance may choose a third-party lobbyist
as its agent. In this arrangement, the lobbyist does not come from any
of the participating groups and hence cannot be accused of favoring
the interests of any single alliance member. Choosing a third-party
lobbyist may have other advantages; he may provide a "smokescreen"
to conceal the identity of the groups in the alliance or, perhaps, regular
lobbyists for the participating groups are too committed to a point of
view and are not flexible enough to work on a particular issue without
damaging their credibility on others. Or, as mentioned earlier, a third-

party lobbyist may have special skills or contacts to make his employment highly desirable.

Interconnections between interest groups, alliances, and third-party lobbyists can, in most cases, only be estimated. What facts exist are difficult to evaluate. For example, major tobacco companies are represented by Earle C. Clements, a registered lobbyist and a former Senator from Kentucky. The Covington-Burling law firm represented the same tobacco companies in hearings before the Federal Trade Commission, yet the same tobacco companies were also members of the Tobacco Institute — which in turn employed the Hill and Knowlton advertising and public relations firm during the cigarette labeling bill controversy.

Similarly, during the 1965 controversy raised by President Johnson's omnibus farm bill (which proposed to shift $250,000,000 in wheat subsidies from the Treasury to be absorbed by the bakeries), the nation's major bakeries formed the Wheat Users Committee to lobby for their interests. The Wheat Users Committee then, in turn, retained the Covington-Burling firm for legal representation.

Staff Personnel of Intergroup Alliances

Little information about intergroup alliances is available but it is even more difficult to gather data regarding intergroup finances, personnel, and leadership. Therefore, much of this section must be regarded as theoretical and as a guide for further research.

Who furnishes staff personnel to conduct a formal alliance's affairs? There are two general answers: if the alliance is sufficiently structured and presumed to be semi-permanent, cooperating groups will subscribe financially to support the creation and maintenance of a separate staff for the alliance. The Tobacco Institute exemplifies such a separate staff. Or, it may be that whichever group serves as the leader of the alliance will assign a portion of its own staff to the alliance — perhaps a departmental manager with necessary assistants and secretarial help, plus, perhaps, one of the group's staff lobbyists.

Alliance staffs tend to be small, since most of the work is neither materially "productive" nor "distributive." That is, no goods or services are produced other than intergroup communiqués, and the telephone and mail systems are the usual distributors of these products. Occasionally, other services will be contracted for or obtained through subscription, including press clipping services, art work, preparation of mailing lists, etc. Because the major function is coordination and stimulation of other groups, and this is the work of the "professionals," the alliance staff usually remains small. Physical facilities already exist in the lobbyist's own association: meeting rooms, secretarial services, telephones, duplicating equipment, etc. Also, the men who assume intergroup roles are already highly professional. Further, they can depend, with some certainty, upon alliance members' voluntary cooperation, and that of their employees. Since an intergroup project (an identical interest) is ordinarily limited in scope — at least compared to managing the NAM, for example — and often involves only a single issue, no large supporting staff is necessary.

Does it make any difference who furnishes the staff for an intergroup alliance? The general answer is: probably not; for, if it did, participating groups would probably insist upon having a "third-party" staff not under the influence of any of the participating groups.

On the other hand, it is possible that with one group furnishing the staff, the resulting product may bear some of the subtle trademarks of the organization that furnished the staff. A Senate committee staff member said he could always tell whether Robert Heiney (National Canners Association) or Clyde Roberts (NAM) had written a paragraph, press release, or speech. "Both guys have a light but serious and straightforward style — no breastbeating or hoorah."

Who pays expenses incurred by the alliance acting as a unit? Who pays staff salaries and expenses? When associations answer such questions, they usually comment that no complicated system is necessary. Everyone involved knows and generally trusts the others, and it is usual that a consensus has already been reached. The procedure seems to be that each participating group is assessed a proportion of expenses according to a formula agreed upon by the participating members. Such formulas are based, for example, upon participating companies' dollar volume of sales, units of production, number of employees, or according to the proportionate value that a participating group places on the outcome of the issue. (Canners might be hurt more by the Hart "Truth in Packaging" Bill than the bottlers, for example; hence their share of an alliance's expenses might be greater.)

Some conception of this system of pro-rated expenses can be gained from reports of lobbying expenses published quarterly in the *Congressional Record*. For example, Earle C. Clements is listed as a lobbyist for six cigarette companies. Under the entry for each of his employers, Clements listed the same receipts ($1,250) and the same expenditures in connection with legislative interests ($1,401).[28] These

---

[28] *Congressional Record*, May 24, 1965, p. 10912. In the third quarter of 1965, Clements reported receipts from each company of $874.99 and expenditures in their behalf of $1,166.88, according to *Congressional Record*, January 10, 1966, p. 58.

figures indicate that expenses for some common purpose of the six cigarette companies are proportioned among the companies on an "equal-shares" basis.

Costs of conducting the Conference of National Organizations* conventions are apportioned on an equal-shares basis among groups attending. It is presumed that expenses of the Greenbrier Conference * are similarly apportioned.

Although an association's budget limits the expenses that can be incurred, many alliance-incurred expenses are undoubtedly written off as "cost of doing business" expenses by the participating companies or associations.

The extent to which this write-off is possible depends upon the alliance's specific actions, pertinent Internal Revenue Service regulations, and advice of company or association counsel. This write-off feature permits an alliance and its members to place part of lobbying costs on the taxpayers, since this expense would otherwise be deducted from the taxable profits of the groups instead of being listed as a legitimately tax-deductible business expense.

Several logical consequences seem to follow when an alliance's staff is made up of personnel from non-participating groups — that is, of experts or third parties hired for that purpose. First, such a procedure is obviously "temporary," even though an alliance goal may take several years to reach. Because the job of these outside parties is temporary, and because it must also be (a) vital and (b) demanding of expert talent, the services of these personnel will be expensive.

Second, a problem of secrecy arises regardless of which member or participating group provides the staff services. No association or business wants its competitors (who are likely to be included in the alliance) to know too much about the former's business. This is also true regarding the revealing of company or association data to a hired third party. Yet, if the alliance is to be effective, the staff must have a certain amount of confidential "inside" information regarding the participants to make the correct arguments, to present the case intelligently, and to safeguard the participants' interests. Thus, the dilemma: both too much and too little inside information is dangerous to the participating groups — but how is a group to draw the line? The assumption is that most groups would tell the alliance staff, "Ask for whatever you think you should know; we'll decide whether or not you should know it."

A third logical consequence of employing an alliance staff from

---

*See Chapter Six.

freely competitive economic system. If price were the only guide, manufacturers might feel free to adulterate products, alleged going-out-of-business sales could destroy other legitimate retail outlets, and consumers would find price savings negated by loss of merchandise quality. Senator Hart, in defense of his "truth in packaging" bill, put it this way:

> The practices with which this bill are concerned do not generally reflect a desire to deceive on the part of the manufacturer. Rather they are a reaction to competitive practices which have made the package the new salesman in the supermarket. If one manufacturer receives a temporary advantage by making his package look bigger while at the same time lowering the content, then the competitor feels he must follow the leader or lose sales. This process has resulted in the follow-the-leader approach to marketing, with the leader sometimes being the least scrupulous in the marketplace . . . By establishing before-the-fact ground rules, this bill would allow the legitimate manufacturer to follow his personal ethical standards without being penalized in the marketplace. . . .[24]

Not all retailers or manufacturers agree with Senator Hart that his bill would stop deceptive pricing and/or packaging. Yet, every industry is concerned with the danger that prices may be determined by unscrupulous methods of the "price dealer."

The National Automobile Dealers Association (NADA) general counsel said in an interview that "the Hart bill won't stop the few bums in our industry — they'll find a way to capitalize on the confusion that would result from credit costs being computed on an annual rate percentage." He pointed out that NADA has developed, in cooperation with the Association of Better Business Bureaus, a series of advertisements directed toward the communications media, urging them to "join us in a fight . . . Our target is the fast buck phoney . . . He destroys believability in advertising . . . [You] possess the . . . power to refuse dishonest advertising." The advertisement closes with an offer to send communications media a free copy of "Recommended Standards of Practice for Advertising and Selling Automobiles." [25]

Self-Regulation Preferred to Government Regulation

The 1965 furor over passage of the Cigarette Labeling Bill was the outcome of two conflicting forces meeting in the congressional

---

[24] Statement by Senator Philip A. Hart (D.-Mich.) on S. 985 (Fair Packaging and Labeling Bill), 1965, mimeographed and distributed by his office.

[25] Interview with Steven Simmerman, General Counsel, National Automobile Dealers Association, Washington, D.C., August 18, 1965. See also NADA, *The Franchised New Car and Truck Dealer Story,* (1965), p. 47.

arena. On one side were the forces of government-supported medicine and many private medical groups: the U. S. Public Health Service, American Cancer Society, American Heart Association, Tuberculosis Association, and the American Public Health Association, all grouped into an organization called The National Interagency Council on Smoking and Health. On the other side were ranged the tobacco and advertising industries. (Full details of this struggle appear in a later chapter.) Congress was placed in the difficult position of being pressured to force the nation to reduce cigarette smoking while at the same time being pressured to avoid offending the subsidized tobacco industry and commercial advertisers and broadcasters.

Prior to arrival of this issue in Congress, the tobacco industry and the advertisers tried to forestall its emergence as a national legislative issue. The tobacco industry and broadcasters developed a Cigarette Advertising Code to be administered by an independent committee under the supervision of ex-Governor Robert Meyner of New Jersey. While the cigarette companies paid expenses of the Code's operation, the committee headed by Meyner had freedom to rule on the suitability of cigarette advertising, with special emphasis on preventing advertising directed toward urging young people to smoke.

Formation of the Cigarette Advertising Code followed by almost a year the announcement by the Tobacco Institute's George V. Allen that "the Tobacco Institute's position [is] that smoking is a custom for adults and that it is not the intent of the industry to promote or encourage smoking among youth," and that "cigarette advertisements should be characterized by good judgment and good taste." [26]

The National Association of Broadcasters, pressured to cooperate with both cigarette advertisers and federal health officials, amended their radio and television codes to read:

Commercials may not convey the impression that cigarette smoking promotes health or is important to the personal development of the nation's youth. In programming, cigarette smoking may not be depicted to impress young people that it is a habit worthy of imitation.[27]

Was this a form of self-regulation to forestall possible government regulation? According to the Association's *Special Report* of 1964 it appears so:

---

[26] Press release by George V. Allen, President of the Tobacco Institute, July 9, 1963.

[27] National Association of Broadcasters, *1964 Major Issues and Projects: Special Report to the NAB Membership* (Washington, D.C.: Fall, 1964), p. 28.

The Radio and Television Codes represent the industry's commitment to the goals of self-regulation. The Codes reflect the view that, "There is no way to claim the virtue of self-regulation without also shouldering its responsibilities." During the year many steps have been taken to further strengthen both Codes through amendments to the Codes, increased enforcement activities, and greater industry support. Efforts to develop public and governmental awareness and understanding of Code activities have been intensified.[28]

How effectively an industry can lobby when threatened with federal regulation because the industry has been unable or unwilling to regulate itself, is shown by attempts of the drug industry to block the Kefauver Bill early in the Kennedy administration:

The drug companies retained the services of a half-dozen law firms that had one thing in common — close ties to the president, or to his associates in the administration.

One of these firms was headed by former Secretary of State Dean Acheson. The senior partners of another firm included Paul Porter, President Truman's OPA administrator, and the newest Supreme Court justice, Abe Fortas, who has been considered notably close to President Johnson. Another firm had prominent alumni in the government itself — George Ball, Undersecretary of State, and Fowler Hamilton, head of the foreign aid program. A partner in still another of the firms was Edward Foley, Undersecretary of the Treasury in the Truman administration and chairman of President Kennedy's inaugural committee . . . .

As the battle over drug laws built up, the White House was reluctant to extend support to Kefauver. On June 6, 1962, a meeting was held in the offices of Sen. James O. Eastland of Mississippi. Representatives of the administration and agents of the drug lobby — including the President's friend, Foley — sat down and drafted a weak substitute for Kefauver's bill. No senators were present.

Kefauver might have lost his fight right there. But then the thalidomide scandal broke and so aroused the country that both White House and Congress switched signals and lined up in favor of the Kefauver bill. It was promptly passed.[29]

In the case of the drug companies, desire for self-regulation had not been strong enough to enforce industry conformity in testing procedures, drug advertising, price increases, and other alleged industry

---

[28] *Ibid.*, p. 25.

[29] Richard Harwood, "Special Interest Groups Have a Way of Collecting," *Louisville Courier-Journal,* October 12, 1965.

abuses that Kefauver's bill was intended to correct. As a result, federal regulations on drugs were strengthened.

If one were keeping score, the drug industry "lost." On the other hand, it is clear that the tobacco companies and advertisers "won" — all that was required of them was an almost unnoticeable warning statement on the side of cartons and packages, a warning the companies and government health officials agreed would not be effective. And, as a bonus, Congress prohibited state and federal agencies from regulating cigarette advertising, in respect to dangers of smoking, for a period of three years. This poses a question: Did the tobacco and advertising industries' ability to put *some* self-regulation into operation promptly have the effect of securing, for them, leniency from Congress?

The answer is probably not that simple. One can draw a comparison between the thalidomide scandal that rocked the drug industry and the Surgeon General's report that rocked the tobacco and advertising industries. But there is little question that the American people are more addicted to cigarettes than to drugs; and there is little question that the cigarette, broadcasting and advertising industries have greater congressional support and liaison than does the drug industry. Part of this congressional support can be traced to the probable fact that more than one-third of the members of Congress own radio or television interests.[30] The lack of competent or "well connected" counsel cannot be the decisive factor in the degree of success, for both the drug industry and the tobacco industry employed the Arnold, Fortas and Porter law firm (among other counsel).

INDUSTRY POSITION CAN NEUTRALIZE GOVERNMENT

Given the federal nature of American government and the separation of powers provided for by the Constitution, one of the preliminary strategy decisions many groups must make is for a group to decide whether to try its case before Congress or the states, before the President or before federal agencies having their own clientele to advance and protect, before politicians or before the public. The interstices in the power structure of American government provide groups with access to a variety of decision-makers. The problem is to determine which "set" will give one's case the most favorable consideration.

---

[30] "Edmund C. Bunker, president of the Radio Advertising Bureau, and a former lobbyist for one of the broadcasting networks, has estimated that more than one third of the members of Congress own radio or television interests." Desmond Smith, "American Radio Today," *Harper's Magazine,* Vol. CCXXIX, No. 1372 (September, 1964), p. 61.

"Keep It in Congress" vs. "Keep It out of Congress"

Three recent legislative issues have been artfully maneuvered by their proponents to make Congress the judge of the outcome. The purpose of the proponents was clear: if Congress pre-empted the dispute, the states could not act in that field except by sufferance of Congress. These issues were the cigarette controversy, the Hart and Douglas "consumer" bills, and the proposed repeal of Section 14(b) of the Taft-Hartley Act.

The motives of the tobacco industry were based on its fear that individual states might be free to impose such regulations on cigarette advertising and labeling that an extensive and expensive mélange of conflicting regulations would result. Further, the tobacco industry realized that the majority of its legislative support lay in a dozen or so states whose combined efforts in key congressional committees could protect tobacco interests. Richard Harwood assessed the situation in this way:

> The industry also can muster voting blocs of up to 150 members in the House and more than 40 in the Senate. Furthermore, no less than 11 committee chairmen in Congress represent tobacco states . . . .
>
> The administration's reluctance to get into the fight meant that Congress was on its own in dealing with one of the biggest public health issues of the 20th century. This is precisely the situation the tobacco lobby was seeking to bring about . . . .
>
> As Bowman Gray, board chairman of R. J. Reynolds Tobacco Co., told the House Commerce Committee: "We do not believe . . . that any governmental action is necessary at the present time with respect to cigarette advertising and labeling. If such measures are to be taken, however, we believe they should be taken by the Congress and by no one else." . . .
>
> [Still quoting Gray] "Any such legislation should make absolutely clear," he said, "that the congressional statute preempts the field. It would be intolerable if the states and federal agencies were to remain free to pass conflicting laws or impose conflicting regulations on this subject."[31]

Supporters of the Douglas "Truth in Lending" Bill and the Hart "Truth in Packaging" Bill made it plain that they did not believe individual states could muster the legislative courage, or independence from influence of large industries within the state, to enable the various legislatures to enact adequate consumer legislation. For this reason,

---

[31] "President Doesn't Switch Nor Fight Tobacco Congressmen," *Louisville Courier-Journal,* October 13, 1965.

The effectiveness of these large scale organizations [national Chamber, NAM] is limited by their overlapping interests and by the lack of cooperation among the associations and among industry generally. As an example, farmers are represented by a number of organizations — the American Farm Bureau Federation, the National Farmers Union, and so forth. But who really speaks for the farmer? And labor is represented by many organizations. But when it comes to the labor movement — in contrast to the business or farm movement — labor is organized vertically, like a pyramid, with most of the power lying at the top. Thus labor's approach on legislative matters can be united and effective. Labor can motivate its auxiliary groups and local organizations. Management and business generally do not have this capacity in their organizational structure — except insofar as branch plants can be motivated by the home office.

I do not think there is any formal mechanism for integrating all the resources of business on one single project. But the thing business has more of than anyone else is a good exchange of information of a highly accurate and technical sort.[21]

There are, of course, jurisdictional problems even within the narrower classification of a single industry. The Support Group for Progressive Banking, for example, is neither admired nor appreciated by the American Bankers Association although the objectives of each group are quite similar.

The American Bankers Association considers the Support Group to be a splinter organization of bankers interested mainly in advancing interests of the national banks.[22] Other divisions within the banking industry exist between national and state bank interests, banks interested in mergers and those that are not, and of course, there is the sharp cleavage and sense of competition between banks and savings and loan companies, small loan companies, and other credit retailers.

Groups With Secrecy as a Problem

Secrecy is a general preoccupation of both lobbies and the persons they pressure. It may be true that lobbies, like ivy, thrive best in the shade. Nevertheless, certain kinds of interest groups have a greater need of secrecy than others. And certain groups, because of the nature of the businesses they represent, would be questionable partners in any

---

[21] Interview with Ernest Tupper, Tupper Associates, Washington, D.C., August 18, 1965.

[22] Based on interviews with William T. Heffelfinger, Federal Administrative Adviser, American Bankers Association, Washington, D.C., June 17, 1965; and Mr. Jack Yingling, Support Group for Progressive Banking, Washington, D.C., June, 1965.

reasonably open alliance. The matter of secrecy, therefore, is a motive limiting some intergroup cooperation.

Racetracks, liquor outlets, gambling houses, and other enterprises skirting the edges of American puritanism have usually found it necessary to lobby state and national legislatures simply to stay in business. Sometimes they must lobby to expand their operations or to prevent being taxed excessively to expiate for their "sins." In this latter regard, the cigarette industry has probably had more taxes levied against its product than any other retail commodity — except gasoline, perhaps, but gasoline taxes are rarely related to American morals. (There have been studies linking automobile availability with promiscuity among teenagers, but the tax problem is not pertinent.)

The point is, few groups openly ally with liquor dealers or gambling syndicates. The presumed weight of public opinion is already against these groups; they operate only by sufferance of legislatures and people addicted to these pleasures. Further, members of the public rarely wish to be confronted with the "wages of sin" (although they accept its taxes). Leaders of such "borderline" groups respond by maintaining the closest secrecy about funds, operating expenses, and staffs.

Secrecy also poses a problem for the group that lobbies for an interest so obviously beneficial to itself alone that it must disguise sponsorship of the group to win support. For example, only a limited number of people stood to benefit to a large extent from H.R. 10, a bill to allow self-employed people to set aside part of their earnings, tax deferred, toward retirement. Certainly, the bill benefited those with higher incomes to a far greater extent than those in lower brackets, although the point can be made that the bill would serve as an incentive to all self-employed persons.

The bill was promoted by the American Thrift Assembly, a largely anonymous group headed by Robert E. Ansheles, a personable if taciturn lobbyist who also represents the Consolidated International Trading Corporation of New York (CITC).[23] Ansheles, according to remarks made by other lobbyists, coordinated the efforts of all those interested in H.R. 10. According to his peers, it was his ability and energy that largely accounted for the passage of the bill.

A third problem posed by the need for secrecy involves large multi-purpose groups such as the national Chamber of Commerce, the NAM, and the Farm Bureau. The problem arises when a member group

---

[23] Ansheles registered as a lobbyist for CITC, according to *Congressional Record*, 89th Cong., 1st Sess. (May 24, 1965), p. 10900. His work for American Thrift Assembly was detailed to the author by a lobbyist for a prominent professional organization headquartered in Washington.

seeks to have its interest adopted by its association or an alliance of associations. Can the smaller group be certain that its interest will not be compromised or made public for the good of the larger group? If multi-purpose groups are to have a unified program, they must reach a compromise of interests. Yet, however small a group sitting as a privy council to make the compromise, this compromise can be reached only by debate and discussion of relevant facts. It is this very airing of the relevant facts, of confidential information, that the worried participant wishes to avoid. Such a group therefore has a strong motive for refusal to cooperate with other interest groups, even a parent association of which the group is already a member.

It should be stressed that the nature of a particular group, determined by its effectiveness, record, image, ideology, leadership, involvement in politics and jurisdictional conflicts, and the need for secrecy, can provide motives for its inability or unwillingness to cooperate with others and vice versa. The nature of these groups cannot be called "good" or "bad" except in relative terms; in this case the terms are generally relative to past successes, the friends they keep, enemies they have made, and whether the groups have legitimate needs for secrecy.

THE PROBLEM OF FEAR

Fear, as a motive against intergroup cooperation, generally has as its object an opposition group, or some agency of government, the press, or a usually ill-defined segment of the public. Of these "fear objects," government and the press generally rank first and second.

Fear of the Opposition

Fear of polarizing the opposition or causing it to coalesce has been discussed as a disadvantage inherent in the formation of alliances. Groups determined to form alliances seek to define their goals and select allies with many strategic considerations in mind, one of which is to avoid alliance with a group whose inclusion would cause the opposition to escalate its efforts against the alliance. David Truman used the example of the Emergency Price Control Act of 1942 to show that Congress avoided including wage ceilings in the act because such a proposal would have cemented an alliance between farm groups (already opposed to the bill) and labor unions (who would become opposed to it if wage ceilings were included).[24] Similarly, it is possible that one of the reasons why the Grocery Manufacturers Association (GMA), one of the most powerful food industry associations, was not

---

[24] Truman, *op. cit.*, p. 366.

a formal member of the Food Group [25] was that the GMA was already a target of the Truth In Packaging Bill's supporters.[26] To include the GMA in the Food Group might have destroyed the Group's effectiveness by drawing too much enemy fire. Discussing this fear of opposition, Truman concluded:

> Given the importance of alliances in the legislative process, a skillful sponsoring group or leader will avoid drafting or interpreting legislation in terms which will facilitate opposing alliances.[27]

It is always possible that fear of the opposition will spur a coalition to greater effort, to fight more fiercely for its objectives. But interest group leaders and their lobbyists discount this possibility and prefer to avoid opposition whenever possible. As practical people, they have little reason to play Galahad or to wish, like Quixote, for new dragons to slay. As one lobbyist said, "We spend most of our time just trying to put out brush fires; you think we look for forest fires?"

Some lobbyists admit that they occasionally have to make the opposition appear more formidable than it really is, otherwise the group's members might decide to cut back on their support or dues. Staff members sometimes refer to this procedure as "the difficulty of keeping the members excited." Clyde Roberts, of the Government Relations Division of the NAM, put it this way:

> All large organizations like ours, where the members' contact with the organization may be infrequent or limited, face the dual organizational problems of keeping our membership excited yet being flexible enough ourselves to be effective on the Hill. The problem here is that the kind of extreme position that may make a group's members happy is the very kind of position or action that does not impress congressmen; while the type of action or propaganda that is likely to be effective with congressmen is not likely to be effective in stirring up the membership to support the position.[28]

---

[25] The Food Group is discussed extensively in a later chapter. Briefly, it is an "informal conference group of Washington, D.C. executives and representatives of associations in the food industries and directly related industries" whose avowed purpose is to provide a forum "for helpful interchange of information and views among its individual members and with officials of government and others . . ." according to the introduction accompanying its membership roster.

[26] See for example "A Story for Our Times," reprinted as a pamphlet from *Consumer Reports* (March, 1965), in which GMA is said to be "at the peak of the pyramid" of the food industry.

[27] Truman, *op. cit.,* p. 366.

[28] Interview, Washington, D.C., August 20-23, 1965.

Apparently Mr. Roberts has succeeded in solving both problems. A source in the national Chamber of Commerce said of the NAM:

It used to be the most dogmatic and uncompromising and intransigent organization in Washington. Their way of operating was to take the most extreme position on an issue that they could possibly justify intellectually. They would use this position to whip up their membership to peaks of fury against the government or against particular congressmen. Then they would go to those congressmen and say "See what our members want us to do? But we're reasonable; let's work out a compromise that's not so extreme. Then we'll sell it to our members as the best we could hope to get."

Now that's all changed. The NAM has worked much harder on trying to make friends with congressmen and the administration instead of trying — like Hoffa used to do — to threaten them into submission. The NAM is definitely getting more "positive," more "flexible." Their members are not demanding as much of the old fire and brimstone as the organization used to put out. Today, the NAM can even get in bed with the administration.[29]

Fear of Congress

If many citizens in America are fearful of the power of lobbies, there are many lobbyists who are fearful of the federal government's power used against them personally or against their group. Government is not at all powerless in dealing with lobbies; the problem lies in what particular means to use, when to use it, and against which particular lobby, its practices or practitioners.

Federal regulations concerning price fixing, reciprocal purchase agreements, and collusion in bidding have limited much of the freedom of business groups desiring to get together to gouge the public. But the two major government weapons are the investigatory and rule-making powers of the Internal Revenue Service (concerning tax exemptions) and the threat or use of the congressional investigation.

Discussing the means by which senators can control pressures brought upon them by lobbyists, Matthews describes the various methods senators can use to influence lobbyists. After "noncooperation," "the friendship ploy," "helping the lobbyists satisfy the lobbyist's constituents," Matthews' list concludes with "attack":

---

29 Interview with present employee of the national Chamber who insisted on anonymity; Washington, D.C., July 23, 1965. This person has had extensive service in three different national organizations. For an excellent treatment of the *beginning* of NAM's new approach, see "Renovation in NAM," *Fortune Magazine,* Vol. XXXVIII, No. 1 (July, 1948), pp. 72-75, 165-69.

Lobbyists are sitting ducks — their public reputation is so low that public attack is bound to be damaging. To invite public attack, or even worse, a Congressional investigation, is, from the lobbyists' point of view, clearly undesirable. Here, then, is the shotgun in the closet. Its recoil may be substantial — efforts to punish lobbyists by publicity often decrease the prestige of the Senate as well as the lobbies — but then, the mere fact of its existence means that it need seldom be used.[30]

The two sordid years of bit-by-bit revelations of the Bobby Gene Baker story [31] proved the truth of Matthews' last remark: the prestige of the Senate suffered more than that of Mr. Baker. Nor had investigation of the Baker affair been completed when the 89th Congress apparently decided it had washed enough dirty linen in public — dirty linen that figuratively came from the Senate's own dining room.

Threat of congressional investigation is still a loaded gun pointed in the general direction of every lobby influential enough to be considered a sporting target. A spokesman for one of the largest drug manufacturing associations said, in relation to the Hart Packaging Bill:

Senator Hart can hold over such organizations as the Proprietary Drug Association, drug manufacturers, advertising agencies, and general media and their publications the threat of senatorial investigation. In fact, our opposition to the Hart Bill might have been more extreme except for the fact that we were "made aware" of this.[32]

Fear of the Internal Revenue Service (IRS)

While congressional investigation, or the threat thereof, may be a shotgun in the closet, the power of the Internal Revenue Service to grant or withhold tax-exempt status for interest groups is the real blunderbuss in the foyer. Mistrust, if not actual fear, of the IRS pervades most of the conversations held with lobbyists and interest group personnel. A selection of quotations follows, with anonymity given those who insisted that they (or their organization) must not be identified — frequently for fear of the IRS.

(1) Our organization has been under investigation by the IRS for over [*] months. During that entire time I have had one or more of

---

[30] Matthews, *op. cit.*, p. 190.

[31] See for example Ben H. Bagdikian and Don Oberdorfer, "Bobby Was the Boy to See," *Saturday Evening Post,* Vol. 236, No. 43 (December 7, 1963), pp. 26-29.

[32] Interview with a member of the Proprietary Association, Washington, D.C., August 16, 1965.

their agents in my offices, going through my files, talking to my employees, and for all I know tapping my own telephone. They've tapped phones before, you know. When I want to make a business call I have to go to a pay phone in the drugstore. Our association's members have stopped coming to the office to talk business *or* pleasure; some of my staff have quit because they think I must be headed for a jail sentence and they don't want to go down with me. So you're not going to get me to talk about your "intergroup cooperation." Why don't you write something about the way the IRS is harassing legitimate business associations? [33]

(2) The fear of being investigated by the IRS is held to some extent by all organizations, and this fear is really based on the fact that the IRS regulations are not too clear to begin with. We don't consider the IRS activity as harassment but rather as a type of surveillance that amounts to — as far as we're concerned — simply interference with our work. However, if business associations are being examined by the IRS, so must be the labor unions, so it doesn't really work to anyone's advantage as far as our legislative effectiveness goes.[34]

(3) The national Chamber of Commerce probably has good reason to be worried about violating the IRS regulations. The primary way in which legislative activities are disguised as normal Chamber activities with their membership is by reporting time spent on legislative affairs at a very minimum, while actually much greater time is spent on these affairs than is reported. For instance, a department may work for a period of weeks on a legislative matter and come up with testimony for several witnesses and a brochure or a pamphlet to be mailed out to the membership. Yet the only time that will show as being devoted to legislative matters is a fraction of the actual time spent on preparing this attempt to influence legislation. This is probably why Arch Booth [Executive Vice President of the Chamber] is worried.[35]

(4) Almost every professional and business association that I know of has recently been audited by the Internal Revenue Service, and this audit procedure has made many of the associations wary of discussing the kind and degree to which they are involved in relations with other groups. What you call "intergroup relations" could be considered by the IRS as time spent on legislative matters, and could add up to enough time, possibly, to make the group into a "principal purpose" group and thereby possibly lose its tax-exempt status.[36]

---

[33] Interview with the director of a large association of retail stores. Anonymity demanded.

[34] Clyde F. Roberts, National Association of Manufacturers, Washington, D.C., August 20-23, 1965.

[35] Interview with former senior employee of the national Chamber. Anonymity demanded.

[36] Warren G. Elliott, Assistant Counsel, Life Insurance Association of America, Washington, D.C., August 24, 1965.

Notice that the first interview quoted reports an organizational handicap — a breakdown of membership-staff relationships — as a result of IRS "interference." The second interview equates IRS activity with "surveillance" rather than harassment and assumes (incorrectly, it appears) that labor and business groups are scrutinized equally. The third interview points out the peculiar viciousness of the ambiguous regulations followed by the IRS: if *no* group knows how much of its time it may spend on discussing legislative strategy with other groups, almost *any* group could be accused of stepping over its quota of permissible lobbying by simply consorting with groups which are already, as lobbying groups, non-exempt.

Lobbyists are not the only ones in Washington to report a "feeling" that they are singled out by the IRS for surveillance or harassment. Senator John J. Williams (R-Del.) reported that his affairs were subjected to a "tedious audit" by the IRS at the time he was leading the investigation of the Bobby Baker case. The IRS denied any attempt at harassment, but Williams said:

Taken alone, I wouldn't think much of it, but the whole series of circumstances, taken together, did raise a question of what was going on.
Members of Congress are not above having their tax returns audited. I'm not complaining about any of the treatment I received, but I do wonder sometimes.[37]

On what factors are these fears of the IRS based? The answer lies in IRS powers to grant, withhold, or revoke the tax-exempt status of lobbying groups. Following passage of the 1946 Federal Regulation of Lobbying Act, authority to grant tax exemptions to non-profit groups was vested in the Exempt Organizations Branch of the Tax Rulings Division of the National Office of the Internal Revenue Service. In some routine cases, a local District Director of Internal Revenue grants these exemptions.

Research, although limited in depth and scope relative to tax treatment of interest groups, nevertheless indicates that the guidelines by which the IRS determines the tax status of a group claiming exemption are vague and have been inconsistently applied, leaving the entire subject in a confused muddle. According to one of the leading tax experts in this field, a partner in the prestigious Washington law firm of Davies, Richberg, Tydings, Landa & Duff:

---

[37] John Barron, "The Case of Bobby Baker and the Courageous Senator," *Reader's Digest*, Vol. LXXXVII, No. 521 (September, 1965), p. 116.

One of the continuing difficulties in the exempt organization area of the Federal tax law has been the inadequate and inept statutory scheme. There are many inconsistencies and deficiencies . . . This situation has been compounded by the Internal Revenue Service. Through the years and without regard to political administrations, the Service has permitted further inconsistencies to arise in the administration of the statute . . . Despite the fact that many organizations serve the public interest, both the statutory grant of exemption and the administration of exemption have been a matter of considerable discrimination . . . .

[The Service appears to have] a labor bias which has no basis whatsoever in the taxing statute . . . This same labor bias has apparently existed in the *administration* of the law by the Service — and with the same lack of statutory support. This bias has been apolitical, for the discrimination has occurred throughout the entire history of the two exemption statutes, and without apparent regard to which political party was in power.[38]

According to regulations promulgated up to and including April 20, 1965, groups may be considered for tax-exempt status provided, among other qualifications, that (a) no *substantial* part of their activities consists of expenditures for lobbying purposes, for the promotion or defeat of legislation, for propaganda or advertising to accomplish these purposes, and that no part of their expenditures or activities consists of support for political campaign purposes or for propaganda or advertising to accomplish these purposes; (b) that activities of the group or the legislation concerning which it is lobbying have a *direct effect* on interests of the group's members, that is, the legislation must be of direct interest to the members of the group, even if of direct interest to only one member of the group; (c) that the group does not receive "unrelated business income" in excess of 30 per cent of the total income of the group — *with the proviso* that the percentage itself is not determinative and that the grant of exemption depends upon a consideration of all relevant factors.[39]

Therefore, if the IRS determines that a substantial part of the

---

[38] G. D. Webster, "Current Inconsistencies and Discrimination in the Taxation of Exempt Organizations," 21 *Journal of Taxation* 102-05 (August, 1964). See also by the same author, *Federal Tax Aspects of Association Activities* (Washington: Chamber of Commerce of the United States, 1962); Mitchell Rogovin, "Exempt Organizations: New Procedures and Current Policies Within the IRS," 20 *Journal of Taxation* 28 (January, 1964); M. Schoenfeld, "Federal Tax Aspects of Non-Profit Organization," 10 *Villanova Law Review* 487 (1965). Rogovin is especially interesting on the subject of steps planned by the IRS to improve its coverage and audits of exempt organizations.

[39] G. D. Webster, *Federal Tax Aspects of Association Activities, op. cit.;* for 1965 changes in IRS regulations see *Federal Register,* Vol. 30, No. 75 (April 20, 1965).

group's activities consists of lobbying or advertising to influence or accomplish the passage or defeat of congressional legislation, the group may lose or be denied a tax-exempt status. As with everything that touches lobbying rules, apparently, the difficulty lies in interpretation of the regulation's wording. What is a "substantial" part of a group's activities? Are the group's activities to be judged on the basis of one year or several years? Is it sound to expect that the IRS can accurately judge when particular legislation "is of such a nature that it will, or may reasonably be expected to, affect the trade or business of the taxpayer [or membership group]"? If the 30 per cent figure of "unrelated business income" cannot be used as a determinative factor in granting or withholding an exemption, what percentage figure can be used? Can any be used?

Apparently the only answer lies in this vague IRS guideline found in the 1965 revised rulings:

The determination of whether a substantial part of an organization's activities consists of one or more of the . . . [proscribed] activities . . . shall be based on all the facts and circumstances.[40]

In short, only the IRS can determine whether an organization has committed acts which jeopardize its tax-exempt status. A particular organization has no way of forecasting what *specific* activities are proscribed other than "too much lobbying," "too much promotion to pass or defeat legislation," "any political campaigning," and "too much advertising of the wrong kind."

Can the IRS determine *in advance* what an organization may not do without violation of the exempt status? Apparently not. The following information was elicited in a telephone interview with the Executive Assistant to the Assistant Commissioner, Compliance Division, Internal Revenue Service:

A percentage can also be very misleading. You can have one organization spend a very small percentage but an awful lot of money. Another very small organization can spend a large percentage but a very small amount of money. And the expense can be a one-time shot or continued. It all depends on the circumstances . . . .

Let's assume that this organization starts issuing pamphlets and they contain both educational and political material. Now, how would you determine, if you were a revenue agent . . . how would you determine what portion of this is "political" and what portion is "educa-

---

[40] Federal Register, *op. cit.*

tional?" I think you would have to count the lines of each. There may be other ways, don't misunderstand me, but an accountant would look at this thing and say "How many lines?" What ways would they [the organizations] suggest? Anyway, that's the way we do it, but I am not saying we are always right. We make many mistakes.

I think that if the law says that you are supposed to operate a certain way, and we [IRS] are exempting you from tax because you do operate this way, then if you do other than what the law is . . . if you don't operate according to your charter, I think you ought to come in and amend that charter and ask for another exemption due to the fact that the circumstances under which you are operating are different — or we then ought to challenge it [the charter or its tax-exempt status].[41]

Later in the interview, Wolfe discussed an audit of the national Chamber of Commerce begun in 1963, still in progress in 1966. According to Wolfe, the Chamber was "not suspect," but because its activities have broad scope it was possible that it may have been engaging in such a number of activities designed to influence legislation as to cause it to lose its tax-exempt status. Wolfe also said there was no percentage or other formula by which the IRS could state exactly what proportion of an organization's activities could be political before losing its tax-exempt status. He said that a small organization might spend 90 per cent of its budget on political affairs and yet the amount of money spent might be only $1,000. A large organization might spend only 10 per cent of its budget and yet the amount may be $600,000 or $6,000,000. Wolfe believed that dollar amounts, as a guide, would also be unworkable, since an organization that spends 90 per cent of its budget on political work — even though the amount were only $1,000 — was obviously a political group; while a large organization's political activities — costing $6,000,000 — would obviously have an effect on legislation even though the dollar figure represented only 10 per cent of the group's budget.

Thus, the same difficulty haunts the IRS as haunted Congress when it passed the Lobbying Act: definition of terms. The Lobbying Act leaves undefined a "principal purpose group," the IRS regulations

---

[41] Singleton Wolfe, August 19, 1965. It should be noted that the McClellan Committee disagreed with the point of view represented in Mr. Wolfe's statement. The committee recommended in its final report (*Senate Report 395/1957, op. cit.,* p. 69) that "more readily determinable criteria [be used] to establish coverage under the Lobbying Act, and that, in general, a dollar-and-cents amount received or spent is superior to the existing [principal purpose] criterion." The committee also reported (p. 74) that the advice it had received from scholars familiar with lobbying indicated that "substantial impact upon the legislative process is much more accurately measured in terms of dollar expenditure than in terms of a percentage of a particular organization's budget."

leave undefined what is "a substantial part" of a group's activities. But the fear that haunts the lobbying groups is not undefined: they are afraid of the IRS and the obscure regulations suspended over the heads of even those organizations which might willingly comply with the the regulations if it could be clearly determined what *is* and what *is not* to be reported.

A senior staff member of one of the nation's largest organizations wrote:

> I have decided to try to explain to you the reason why I cannot answer all of the questions in your letter of [*].
>
> Perhaps you have to live in Washington, or have been badgered by the IRS to appreciate the reasoning. But, let me assure you it's real, not fictitious. Our Association is now and has been for the last [*] years under audit by the IRS. We are being audited on our legislative activities and our so-called "unrelated income" producing activities. It is costing us a lot of time, money, and effort to handle the barrage of questions and daily visits, in order to exonerate ourselves.
>
> Now, if I, without all the facts, attempted to answer your letter with respect to legislative and so-called lobbying activities, and name those who are registered or not registered, I am afraid I would be doing our membership an injustice. An injustice because if this letter were made public and did not jibe 100% with the thinking of our "resident" IRS agent, I would have created a problem, not solved one.
>
> The government is great at misconstruing the facts, and therefore I can't attempt to answer your letter without fear of misrepresentation.[42]

It is not, therefore, the Lobbying Act that serves as the effective tool for regulation of lobbying activities. The lobbies are, as are crime syndicates, more afraid of the IRS than of the Justice Department. The lobbies admit that the Lobbying Act has not affected their activities seriously.[43] But the IRS affects the daily operations of interest groups far more directly. If a group loses its tax-exempt status, two things happen automatically: the group must pay taxes on any profits it may make, and group members can no longer deduct membership dues and assessments from their income taxes, (or can no longer deduct that

---

[42] Letter to the author from an association official who insisted on anonymity. Asterisks represent information deleted to protect the identity of the writer. The letter was written in 1965.

[43] "Question 2. Has the fact that there is a statute requiring registration and reports on lobbying activities inhibited or otherwise affected your activities? [Answered by 83 organizations filing reports under the Lobbying Act]: Yes — 5; No — 69; No comment — 9." Questionnaire of November, 1955, in connection with S. 2308, a bill to amend the Lobbying Act; reported in *Senate Report 395/1957, op. cit.,* p. 77.

part of their dues spent on proscribed activities). The former consequence matters little in the long run, for most lobby groups do not make
much profit. Furthermore, if a profit seems imminent, the group can
always spend the excess before the end of the tax year. But if dues
to the group are declared nondeductible, many groups fear that their
income from dues would plummet drastically.

Opinion is not unanimous, however, on desirability of the tax-
exempt status. As one authority has pointed out:

It may be more favorable from a cash standpoint not to have a
tax exemption. Thus, without a tax exemption, an association may
engage vigorously and with no tax restrictions in a magazine, trade
show, etc. [and lobbying].

It enables an association to operate more fully for the benefit of
its membership, without being concerned about or harassed in respect
to activities which help members, but which may be frowned upon by
the [Internal Revenue] Service (such as trade shows, publications,
etc.).[44]

Directors of several lobbying organizations, including officials of
major importance in the national Chamber of Commerce, expressed
this viewpoint to the author. But the majority of groups still feel that
fewer membership dollars would come into group coffers if dues were
not tax-deductible. Those who felt that a loss of tax-exempt status
would not hurt the group stated that, in their opinion, the group would
be better off because "then we could go out and fight like hell and to
hell with the IRS."

One such group, determined to continue lobbying for what it considered to be "in the public interest," lost its privileged tax status as
a direct result of its "substantial" lobbying activities.

On the day following publication in New York and Washington
newspapers of a full page advertisement placed by the Sierra Club, in
opposition to proposed Colorado River dams, the Internal Revenue
Service issued a "warning" to the club that contributions to it would
no longer *necessarily* be tax deductible and that the future tax status
of the club would depend upon "factual determination" of the club's
activities. Should the activities of the club be determined to consist in
"substantial" part of propaganda or other attempts to influence legislation — i.e., lobbying — the IRS would revoke the tax privileges of the
club *and its contributors* as of the date of the warning. As explained
by Sheldon S. Cohen, Commissioner of the IRS, "The Sierra Club set

---

44 Webster, *Federal Tax Aspects of Association Activities, op. cit.,* p. 5a.

diverse groups; others are subcommittees of existing organizations. The distinguishing characteristic of the ad hoc group in each case is that it is formed for a particular purpose, or cluster of purposes. When the purpose is accomplished, the group usually disbands or becomes dormant until another issue affecting the constituent groups arises. However, some ad hoc groups develop into permanent organizations because of (1) the continuing nature of the issue, (2) solidification of common interests of the constituent groups, (3) custom or inertia, (4) a dominant personality as a leader — that is, some person who desires to retain his power, influence, or "glory" as leader of the ad hoc group.

Although not all ad hoc groups are coalitions or alliances, the term "ad hoc" as used here refers solely to ad hoc groups that are coalitions of representatives from several independent organizations. Thus, as an example, a special project committee formed only of national Chamber of Commerce Labor Relations Committee members would not be termed an ad hoc group. On the other hand, a group composed of representatives from the NAM, the national Chamber of Commerce, and the National Small Business Association would be considered an ad hoc group, even though its objective (to conduct a special project in labor relations) and its operations (frequent meetings, preparation of reports) were identical with those of the Chamber subcommittee. (These two groupings are hypothetical examples.)

The organizational form of an ad hoc group varies widely, depending generally upon the purposes and resources of the groups forming the organization. Leadership will often be held by a representative of whatever association first called the ad hoc group into being; but subsequent membership changes may vest leadership in a representative of a group only recently admitted.

Leadership in ad hoc groups, as in other forms of alliances, depends[17] upon such factors as:

1. The degree of commitment a participating organization is willing, or can afford, to give. (Furnishing personnel for the group, making financial contribution, utilizing established contacts, providing office space, etc.)
2. The nature and amounts of power held by the participating groups. (Group size, number of members, geographical distribution of members, degree of access to key decision-makers concerned with the particular issue, etc.)
3. The personality and reputation of the representative from

---

[17] According to a survey of organizations conducted by the author.

each participating group, and the degree to which that representative can commit his group.

4. Other commitments each participating group has.

5. Negative motives preventing group cooperation, as discussed earlier.

6. Each group's familiarity and knowledge concerning the particular issue.

7. Experience of each group in previous efforts to resolve similar issues, and whether a group has been successful in its handling of such issues; also, whether a participating group has become "too well known" in the field to be able to handle the issue with diplomacy and without being limited by previous positions or commitments.

According to a spokesman for one business group which frequently cooperates with other organizations, "Ad hoc groups are usually run by whoever started the group in the first place. In other words, there is no particular reason why one person or group should head it. Rather it seems that when a group gets sufficiently interested in a situation that seems to require legislative action that association or corporation or person will call people he knows to have an interest in the same subject and this initial group will later possibly expand into a larger group, but still under the leadership of the person with the original interest. Frequently whoever first finds out about a particular issue coming up will call the first meeting — that is, if his group wants to get involved."[18]

In most ad hoc groups there is a designated chairman or leader (sometimes self-designated), a formal or informal title, a designated spokesman (if the group operates at all publicly), and a roster of current and potential members.

Scheduled meetings at regular intervals and stipulated dues or contributions are occasionally part of the group's organizational procedures; constitutions, by-laws, and a full complement of officers (secretary, treasurer, etc.) are usually not part of the group's structure.

Ad hoc groups do not, as a rule, keep detailed records or issue formal reports, except that the group's chairman may keep minimum files in his own office. As to why these groups maintain few records or minutes of meetings, one business group representative said: "There is really no need for formal notes or reports of these meetings — you can carry in your hat the guts of what was done or said."[19] The same

---

[18] Interview with Herbert Liebenson, National Small Business Association, Washington, D.C., August 25, 1965.

[19] *Ibid.*

representative then exhibited a copy of a typical report from an ad hoc group's meetings. The report was a recapitulation of a meeting of the [* *][20] Association, an ad hoc group of approximately twenty associations concerned with tax and depreciation problems.

The report listed, item by item, points upon which there was general consensus among groups at a meeting. The report then asked each individual association to suggest alternatives to the points agreed upon, or strategy discussed. The report ended with the statement: "It seemed to be the sense of the meeting that no special groups or task forces should be formed at this time."

Participants in ad hoc groups claim that such groups have distinct advantages over other organizational forms. Ad hoc groups usually have a high degree of informality, an absence of parliamentary rules, and a sense of common purpose permitting open discussion and rapid decisions. They can meet on short notice and can "stay with fast-breaking problems." Like federations, ad hoc groups can expand geographical membership coverage, resources available, and the manpower necessary to cope with serious issues. Most important, ad hoc groups are usually composed of organizations which already recognize that they have a direct and important interest in the issue. Tangential and disruptive interests are thus reduced to a minimum, although conflicts of interest may still arise.

Disadvantages of ad hoc organizations also stem from the group's informality. No group discipline exists since no "punishment" exists — apart from incurring the ill will of other participants. Second, although rapid decisions are possible, there are no binding "majority votes," since each participating group participates voluntarily. Hence, there is no procedural way to end a disagreement except by unanimous decision.

Third, decisions of an ad hoc group — as is the case in a federation — must be executed by units participating (unless a front group is set up). Effectiveness of the ad hoc group is thus limited by the individual effectiveness of a multiplicity of groups disagreeing on all but the one interest represented by the ad hoc group. Because of these other interests, members may not be able to fully commit their groups to the ad hoc group objective or give it primacy.

Fourth, no real locus of responsibility exists. Therefore, responsibility — like membership — must be voluntarily assumed and executed.

Fifth, unless a front group or "task force" is set up by the ad hoc group, or unless the ad hoc group organizes more formally, all staff work will have to be distributed among diverse participating units. This

---

[20] Anonymous at Mr. Liebenson's request.

can create possible conflicts of interest between the participating group's primary interest and the work it assumes as part of its membership in the ad hoc group.

An example of an ad hoc group based upon a continuing common interest was the Ad Hoc Committee on Copyright Law Revision, formed to secure revisions in federal copyright laws.

Represented on the Ad Hoc Committee are such nationally influential organizations as the American Council on Education, the Council of Chief State School Officers, and the National Education Association and many of its affiliates, as well as more specialized groups such as the American Association of Teachers of Chinese Language and Culture and the New Jersey Art Education Association. The National Catholic Welfare Conference and the National Catholic Educational Association are also represented, and Harold E. Wigren, an NEA consultant on educational television who serves as chairman of the Ad Hoc Committee, proudly describes it as "one of the most outstanding examples of the ecumenical spirit in all educational history." [21]

The thirty-five educational organizations composing the Ad Hoc Committee were opposed by two other large groups: the American Book Publishers Council and the American Textbook Publishers Institute, each with more than one hundred members.

The basic question under dispute was, how much freedom educational institutions and instructors require to reproduce materials copyrighted by authors and publishers, provided the materials are used solely as part of classroom instruction or homework. The educators wanted wide latitude in copying such copyrighted material; the publishers and authors "simply want[ed] payment for use of their materials so that they could keep on producing them." [22]

Although the controversy began during the 88th Congress, neither side was willing by the end of that Congress, to compromise sufficiently to agree to one set of copyright law revisions. In reflection of their disagreement, Congress did not complete the revisions both sides agreed were necessary to bring the law up to date. But during the 90th Congress, some agreement was reached and the law was revised in accord with most requests of the educators.

_____

[21] Erwin Knoll, "Our 'Model T' Copyright Law," *Reporter,* Vol. XXXIV, No. 5 (March 10, 1966), pp. 40-41. © 1966, Reporter Magazine Co., by permission.

[22] *Ibid.,* p. 41. See also *CQ, Legislators and the Lobbyists* (2nd ed., 1968) for the role of jukebox and music publishers' and performers' associations.

United Fronts As Ad Hoc Groups

United front organizations almost inevitably have ad hoc structure because groups are rarely able to maintain unity for long on any issue. But, unlike ad hoc groups, united fronts usually have a more formal organizational structure, enabling them to cope with the difficulties of maintaining a united position.

Within a week after introduction of H.R. 9903, a bill to exempt railroads and water carriers from "having their rates for hauling certain commodities regulated by the Interstate Commerce Commission (ICC),"[23] the National Coal Association assumed leadership of the bill's opposition, calling together a meeting of interested groups to coordinate strategy. "A meeting in Washington February 11 [1964] resulted in the formation of the 'Anti-Monopoly Transportation Conference,' whose declared purpose was united 'outright opposition' to the bill." The chairman of the Conference was Robert E. Lee Hall, vice president of the National Coal Association; a vice president representing the waterways operators and a twelve-member board completed the organization's structure. "Policy and procedural decisions by the Conference were made only after consultation with its board of directors or with Washington representatives of Conference members."

The Conference met February 19, 1964, for strategic planning of the united front. As reported by the Conference newsletter, the strategy was threefold: (1) to persuade the House Rules Committee that the bill was controversial and that no rule should be given the bill permitting it to go to the House floor, or, failing that, the bill should be recommitted to the House Interstate and Foreign Commerce Committee for further hearings; (2) to "inform individual Representatives of the damaging effects of the bill on business . . ."; and (3) to "request Senators to see that full and complete hearings are held if the measure passes the House."

By the end of April, the Conference had increased its membership to include fifty-eight groups representing the coal industry, water carriers, maritime interests (both union and management), river basin developers, mining and mineral interests, the Milwaukee Board of Harbor Commissioners, one motor carrier group, and several smaller groups representing shippers. "Notably absent [except for a lone member] from Conference membership were the motor carriers," who regarded H.R.

---

[23] This quotation, those immediately following, and details of the controversy concerning H.R. 9903 are from Congressional Quarterly Service (*CQ*), *Legislators and Lobbyists* (Washington, D.C.: *CQ*, 1965), pp. 68-73.

9903 as less objectionable than other bills pending on the same subject.

Primary opposition to the Conference came from the Association of American Railroads which saw H.R. 9903 as an attempt to "provide equal competitive opportunities in the common carrier transportation industry"; that is, to favor the railroads' competitors.

Although the Johnson administration indicated its willingness to accept several major compromises modifying the bill, the Conference front maintained its united opposition. Their pressure was eventually successful. The House Rules Committee refused the bill a rule (by a 7-8 vote) April 28, 1964. Following the vote, Conference Chairman Hall told *CQ* that "the Conference, its primary mission accomplished, would not dissolve but would work with other common carriers towards 'constructive' legislation in 1965."

In spite of the demonstrated success of some united fronts, interest groups often express strong opposition to the united front as a means for accomplishing intergroup goals. The basis of their negative feelings apparently stems from concern about possible unfavorable reactions to such fronts. According to some, united fronts tend to produce unfavorable reactions among members of Congress, executive agencies, the press, among the groups' own members and the general public. Staff members of the national Chamber of Commerce are especially wary of being considered members of a united front although, as mentioned earlier, the Chamber may be more wary of the Internal Revenue Service than of negative reactions to participation in united fronts.

How justified are these fears of negative reaction? There is little information detailing public reaction. The press seems to take no more interest in a united front than in other forms of lobbying. The membership of most groups usually does not know, or doesn't care, whether a group is part of a united front or any other kind of intergroup cooperation.

There is evidence that executive agencies and congressmen have ambivalent attitudes toward united fronts. As Knoll points out, proposals agreed upon by both sides of a controversy normally are favorably regarded by congressmen—provided the congressmen's constituent interests are not in conflict; and if no such agreement develops, the proposal is likely to fail.

Congress has little appetite for settling the dispute between educators and publishers with a solution that would incur the wrath of either side. When the House hearings were concluded . . . the subcommittee expressed hope that the months of Congressional

adjournment would be used [by the publishers and educators] to work out a compromise . . . .[24]

On the other hand, agencies and congressmen often resent what seems to be a "power play" designed to force agreement to a policy against their wishes. In response to a question whether he was more likely to listen to a united front or to a single lobbying organization, Senator Joseph Clark (D-Pa.) said: "Oh, I don't think it makes much difference. You listen to those groups that come to see you and you make up your own mind. But no senator likes to be in the position of being pressured by a coalition."[25]

A statement by former Senator Paul Douglas (D-Ill.) agrees with that of Senator Clark, to some extent, but adds a further observation: "Of course I am impressed by a united front—provided they really do speak for the groups they claim to represent. And united fronts make it easier for congressmen to vote in committee.

"But I am more impressed by how a group or front responds to cross-examination in committee hearings. It is this cross-examination that improves the quality of testimony, statements, and hearings generally."[26]

Discussing lobbying on Senate Joint Resolution 2, the Dirksen proposal to permit state legislatures to apportion one of their houses on grounds other than population, the Minority Counsel for the Senate Subcommittee on Constitutional Amendments said: "I don't think it makes much difference whether lobbyists come to see you as a united front or as representatives of their individual lobbies. I think most senators would prefer to confront a united group rather than to confront a lot of groups that are in conflict with each other.

"But this only applies when the conflicting groups represent voters within the senator's own state. A senator doesn't have to worry much if the conflicting groups aren't representing his own constituents.

"And senators can easily resent the pressure brought to bear by any coalition. I think you'd have to say that senators are ambivalent on this point.

"Freshmen senators are more likely to be swayed by lobbyists than are seasoned veterans. I ought to know—I used to be a lobbyist myself, for my own business (a fluor spar mining company)."[27]

---

[24] *Op. cit.*, p. 41.
[25] Interview, Washington, D.C., August 10, 1965.
[26] Interview, Washington, D.C., August 26, 1965.
[27] Interview with Clyde Flynn, Washington, D.C., August 11, 1965.

Additional evidence is required before any generalization can be made about effectiveness of united fronts, reaction to them, and attitudes held by groups toward participation in united fronts. All that can be justifiably said at this point is that united fronts occasionally are successful and they occasionally fail; groups join or refuse to join fronts for their own reasons; congressmen appreciate but occasionally resent united fronts; the press is no more interested in, in favor of or opposed to, united fronts than other lobbying activities. The public and the membership of most groups know and care relatively little about united fronts.

The Advisory Committee

The advisory committee—another form of interest group organization has—like ad hoc groups—an indefinite life span determined by its usefulness to those creating it. Several types of advisory committees and their major characteristics will be discussed here.

Advisory commissions, boards, committees, and councils are devices to bring pressure groups and government together as partners in decision-making . . . The advice rendered by such groups affects policy on national, state, and local levels. . . .

A standard pattern of administrative behavior . . . is to obtain support for a desired program by building an "internal constituency" within the government and an "outside constituency" from some segment of the public at large . . . Advisory commissions with representation from both the legislature and pressure groups span the two different constituencies.[28]

Advisory commissions tend to suffer from the same difficulty plaguing regulatory committees: commissions are often overloaded with representatives of the industry concerned and deficient in the number of representatives of the public interest. As Anderson points out: "The Business Council—formerly the Business Advisory Council—in the Department of Commerce, for example, is staffed by large corporate interests who in effect 'screen' ideas on economic policy. The National Petroleum Council in the Interior Department is composed of executives of the major oil companies, and the Federal Advisory Council to the Board of Governors of the Federal Reserve System is constituted entirely of bankers."[29]

---

[28] Totton J. Anderson, "Pressure Groups and Intergovernmental Relations," *The Annals* (American Academy of Political and Social Science), Vol. CCCLIX (May, 1965), p. 121.

[29] *Ibid.* See also Grant McConnell, *Private Power and American Democracy* (New York: Alfred A. Knopf, 1966), pp. 255-80, for a thorough discussion of advisory committees, especially the Business Advisory Council.

It is interesting that this same Business Council was the subject of a protest by the House Special Government Information Subcommittee of the Committee on Government Operations. In the 84th and 85th Congresses this committee criticized the "easy blanket of security" covering "relations between the Government and private advisory committees."[30] Early in the 87th Congress, the Secretary of Commerce responded to this criticism by ordering the Business Advisory Council to open its minutes to the Department of Justice for review. The Secretary of Commerce also pledged "that Council sessions addressed by government officials would not be secret" (H. Rept. 1257, 87th Cong., pp. 29-33). But the committee ruefully reported in 1963:

Subsequent developments all but vitiated the commendable stand taken by the Secretary of Commerce. The Business Advisory Council changed its name, moved into private quarters, and resumed its practice of meeting in secret, hearing secret addresses by Government officials, and even meeting with the President in secret. The only explanation offered for these policies was the argument that private groups have the right to meet in private.

The advisory committee has also been called "the fountainhead of most ersatz employment." In his article on this subject, Don Oberdorfer reported that the Department of Interior alone contained forty-nine advisory committees and commissions "with a total membership of eight hundred citizens, none of whom are subject to Senatorial confirmation or civil-service regulations. Some of these committees are prestigious and powerful, such as the National Petroleum Council, an organization of ninety oil and gas industrialists who influence government petroleum policy from this privileged sanctuary within the gates."[31]

Oberdorfer points out that many advisory committee positions are "non-jobs" in which the appointee has little to do but garner a great deal of prestige. On the other hand, some advisory committees,

---

[30] U. S. House of Representatives, Committee on Government Operations, *Availability of Information from Federal Departments and Agencies,* [House Report No. 918], 88th Cong., 1st Sess., November 22, 1963 (Washington, D.C.: Government Printing Office, 1963), p. 138. This quotation and the matter immediately following are taken from the cited House Report 918. For an example of a "labor advisory group," see references to the President's Advisory Committee on Labor-Management Policy, in *NAM Reports,* Vol. X, No. 20 (May 17, 1965), p. 3. The article concludes that the Committee's members "presumably . . . are among the first to whom the President turns for advice on labor matters."

[31] "The New Political Non-Job," *Harper's Magazine,* Vol. CCXXXI, No. 1385 (October, 1965), p. 110.

such as the Petroleum Council mentioned above, have great influence in shaping, or lobbying for, important public policy.

Reporting on another use of the advisory committee, news reporter Richard Harwood wrote that on April 25, 1963, the Business Committee for Tax Reduction was formed as "a 'front group' for the President of the United States." [32] Co-founders included Henry Ford II, chairman of the Ford Motor Company, and Stuart T. Saunders, chairman of the Pennsylvania Railroad, who also served as the committee's co-chairmen. This committee was organized after a March conference with Secretary of the Treasury Douglas Dillon and Under Secretary Henry Fowler during which they revealed "they were interested . . . in setting up an organization of leading business and financial figures who would be willing to lobby for the Administration's $11.5 billion tax cut plan, which was then headed toward an uncertain fate in Congress."

By January, 1964, "the committee could claim 2,800 members from every state in the union." The committee's main lobbying effort "consisted of nothing more than a few friendly telephone calls and letters to key members of Congress from the committee's business and financial tycoons." Harwood reported that effectiveness of the committee's lobbying effort was "unmeasurable, as an isolated factor," but then added: "Needless to say, however, the tax bill was passed—in complete contradiction to all economic concepts of Congress, including the concept of a balanced budget." [33]

The Business Committee for Tax Reduction was a White House lobby, according to Harwood, but as he also pointed out: "Not all White House lobbies come into existence at the suggestion of the Administration. Instead, they are sometimes formed independently and only later develop close relationships with the President."

Such a lobby, according to Harwood, was the National Council of Senior Citizens, extremely active in lobbying for Medicare and in the 1960 campaigns of President Kennedy and Vice President Johnson (under the name, "Senior Citizens for Kennedy and Johnson").

As the fight over "Medicare" lagged in 1961 and early 1962, the Council and the Kennedy Administration drew closer together. Reg-

---

[32] The information concerning the Business Committee for Tax Reduction and the following account of the National Council of Senior Citizens are from the personal notes of Richard Harwood, Washington reporter for the *Louisville Courier-Journal,* made available to the author in Washington, D.C., August, 1965.

[33] This account of the Business Committee for Tax Reduction is confirmed by James Deakin, a Washington correspondent for the *St. Louis Post-Dispatch,* in his book *The Lobbyists* (Washington, D.C.: Public Affairs Press, 1966), pp. 47-48.

ular meetings were set up between Council representatives and members of the White House staff, principally Kenneth P. O'Donnell . . . and Lawrence F. O'Brien, chief White House lobbyist at the Capitol. At these meetings, according to Dr. Blue Carstenson, [34] basic legislative strategy was agreed upon, information exchanged, and the Council was supplied by O'Brien with the names of "congressmen who were wavering." For its part, Carstenson said, the Council offered suggestions to O'Donnell and O'Brien on "things we thought that the Administration should be doing."

Harwood further reports that the major success of the Council was gaining President Kennedy's support for a nationwide rally of the elderly in behalf of Medicare. The President reluctantly agreed to speak at the lead rally in Madison Square Garden on May 21. In other cities, the Council's rallies featured the Vice President, four cabinet members, thirteen federal administrators "of the highest rank," three senators and two congressmen as speakers. Whatever the effect of these rallies and the campaign by the National Council of Senior Citizens, the Medicare bill became law.

Effect of Organizational Form on Intergroup Lobbying

The question is pertinent whether organizational form has definite effects on the style or procedures of intergroup lobbying. Only a few generalizations are possible, and these do *not* apply to all organizations or all situations.

It is probably true that unitary organizations find it easier to ally with other groups than do federated organizations. The unitary organization has no need to consider the wishes of any component groups; its management can fully commit the group's resources and personnel. But it may also be true that federated organizations are the better allies to have, for they usually have larger membership better distributed geographically.

No significant reasons appear why either vertical or horizontal organizations should find it easier to ally with other groups, or why

---

34 Dr. Carstenson served as executive director of the Council. Also, according to the *Congressional Record* (May 24, 1965, p. 10911), Dr. Carstenson was registered as a lobbyist for the Farmer's Educational and Cooperative Union of America (the National Farmer's Union), a group with close ties to the AFL-CIO. A further example of the close ties between the Council and AFL-CIO, revealed by Harwood, was a letter dated June 13, 1961, from James C. O'Brien of the United Steelworkers Union to Jake Clurman, head of the Industrial Union Department of the AFL-CIO. In this letter O'Brien proposed a $100,000 first-year budget for the Council and a $75,000 second-year subsidy, to be supplied *in toto* by the AFL-CIO. As Harwood's personal notes stated, "The relationship between the Council and the unions, in short, is intimate. That has been true of the relationship between the Council and the White House."

other groups would consider one or the other as a more valuable ally, simply considering organizational form alone.

Ad hoc groups, like united fronts and, frequently, advisory committees, are intergroup alliances with narrowly defined purposes. They tend to work toward a specific goal and disband when the goal is attained or when a group loses its usefulness to its creators.

The size of a group may be either an advantage or disadvantage to potential allies. A large group may be sought for its numerical strength, or avoided because of difficulties in reaching consensus among its members. A large federation may be sought as an ally because of its geographical coverage and ability to mobilize grassroots pressure, or avoided because of a general tendency of federations to take only non-controversial positions on major issues, in order not to jeopardize unity of the federation.

Small groups have the general advantage of ease and rapidity in making decisions, but they are likely to be poorly financed and understaffed. Personnel and funds available for research or operations are limited; the outlook of the group may also be. Geographical coverage and grassroots lobbying potential are limited. (On the other hand, one well-respected constituent may be all that is needed to sway a congressman's vote.)

In short, there seems to be no intrinsic advantage to any one form of group organization. Much like golf irons, there is a shape available to fit the specific "shot" needed. Regardless of the form adopted, groups depend for success upon leadership, circumstances, and operations of the opposition much more than on any advantages that may be inherent in organizational form.

INTERNAL DEMOCRACY AS A FUNCTION OF ORGANIZATIONAL FORM

Rather than ask, "How much and what kind of internal democracy exists within a given organization?" it is more pragmatic to determine how much and what kind of internal democracy *is possible* in a particular group, given the minimum amount of cohesion necessary for the group to function, or desired as part of its organizational policy.

Truman believes that the basis of cohesion, or lack of it, does not lie in the organization's form:

It is the competing claims of other groups *within* a given inter-

Asked about the close association between the National Consumers League and labor organizations, Mrs. Newman said that the
Consumers League had always worked for both consumer legislation
and fair labor standards; she added:

The political effectiveness of the consumer clearing house, like
the Consumers League, comes from their distribution of the information to large organizations, like unions, which do not have consumer
interests as a major objective but which will work for consumer interests if it is made easy for them. The power of the Consumers League
lies in getting other organizations, especially unions, to exert their political pressure in behalf of the Consumers League program. The League
also works through state consumers leagues to see that congressmen
and senators are elected who are sympathetic to consumer legislation
programs.

The packaging industry organized its own clearing house to oppose
the Hart Bill. According to Mrs. Newman's information, the chief
opposition to the Hart Bill came from the Grocery Manufacturers
Association: "Through their control of national advertising [supposedly
based on the large sums spent on advertising by members of the Associ-
ation], they can exert probably the maximum amount of influence. We
always have the NAM and the Chamber of Commerce on the same
side against us, but in this case they were probably not effective."

This description of the major opponents of the Hart Bill is not,
however, consistent with other reports.

A staff member of the Senate Commerce Committee commented,
"The packaging industry had a very active and well-managed coordina-
ting committee, headed by Clyde Roberts of the NAM and Robert
Heiney of the National Canners Association. Their testimony was well
coordinated and so was their letter writing campaign. The entire packaging industry stood together on this bill. To my knowledge not a single
member of the industry swerved from total opposition to the bill;
there was no testimony filed with this committee that would indicate
that any industry supported the bill."[27]

This view is confirmed by business interest groups' staff members
and in a letter from the Information Committee on Federal Food
Regulations which noted "Opposition from the industry has remained
solid and uncompromising."[28]

Actual coordination within the packaging industry, during early

---

[27] Interview with Michael Pertschuk, Washington, D.C., August 11, 1965.
[28] Letter to membership, July 2, 1965.

opposition to the Hart Bill, was accomplished by the "All Industry Packaging Committee," a group whose membership is not generally known but which enlisted Clyde Roberts of the NAM as its chief "trouble-shooter." The All Industry Packaging Committee operated as a non-public united front and successfully enforced as much uniformity of industry position as can be accomplished in a voluntary association. Industry uniformity was believed to be essential in the Hart Bill struggle because the Senate Commerce Committee once successfully split industry uniformity by adopting amendments to the bill, mollifying some major opponents. Once the opposition was split, the Senate Committee pointed to a lack of agreement in the industry and insisted that its own version be accepted. The bill in this case, however, failed to reach the Senate floor.

The summit conference form of organization is distinctive in that its only activity is to conduct a conference or convention at which major groups or associations are exposed to information and argument.

These conferences can be open or closed to the public (but usually are closed) and they also may, or may not, make reports of their deliberations available to the public. (Two of the most important business-association summit conferences, the Greenbrier Conference and the Conference of National Organizations, will be examined later.)

Summit groups may decide to create a continuing association to carry on a long-term or continuous project. Such a resulting association may also be described as a "spin off" ad hoc group, providing it is clear that the new group results from deliberations of a summit group and not merely from the wishes of similarly minded associations. The Information Committee on Federal Food Regulations, stemming from the Food Group, is an example of this kind of continuing subgroup formed to continue opposition as long as the danger lasts. In a July 2, 1965, internal newsletter, the Information Committee notified its members of the necessity to maintain their positions: "For the time being, the subject [the Hart Bill] is on ice. This, however, should not suggest that opponents of additional packaging and labeling legislation also should go into cold storage. Your Washington steering group recommends that now would be a very appropriate time to invite another exchange of correspondence with members of the Senate."

In summary, these summit groups are composed of what F. W. Riggs would call "peak associations" that act as "catalytic groups." [29] They are the leading associations in their fields, are well-financed and know

---

29 F. W. Riggs, *Pressures on Congress: A Study of the Repeal of Chinese Exclusion* (New York: King's Crown Press, 1950).

how to produce the most effective kinds of pressure at the most crucial points. Lines of communication with each other are always open and always active. In taking a strong position on a bill, they are often able to enlist the support of many associations bordering the summit group. For example, during Medicare controversies, the American Medical Association and its summit allies were able to enlist the support of hospital, dental, and nursing associations as well as that of pharmaceutical manufacturers and suppliers, and manufacturers of surgical instruments.

The major limitation affecting these summit groups' operations is the difficulty of achieving unanimity on major issues even when these issues strongly affect the groups' own industry. For example, banks, savings and loan companies, life insurance companies, and small loan companies would all be affected by the Douglas "Truth in Lending" Bill, but banks would tend to benefit while small loan companies could suffer. Thus, the American Bankers Association has not been able to form a summit group to manage the Douglas Bill issue. Coordinated opposition to the Douglas Bill has been developed outside major associations, in ad hoc groups with only one paramount interest, i.e., defeat of the Douglas Bill. In these ad hoc groups, such as the Chamber of Commerce's Credit Study Group and the NRMA's Special Credit Mailing List Group, the ability of the larger associations to control the alliance diminishes as the size and power of the ad hoc group grows.

WAYS OF REACHING CONSENSUS

The most difficult challenge in probing and documenting pressure groups is discerning methods by which groups reach consensus upon what position to take. There simply are not one or two methods of arriving at a consensus. Further, consensus may exist on the national level of associations while their local components may be in violent disagreement. One can only make hypothetical statements, since in virtually no cases is a clear statement of "how we reached agreement" forthcoming from personnel of any association.

However, an incisive statement on methods of achieving intergroup cooperation and consensus follows, made by the Assistant Director of the Washington office of the American Bar Association:

Intergroup cooperation is a nebulous thing you just can't document. It involves personal friendships, personal antagonisms, casual meetings, miscellaneous bits and pieces of information, and a sort of "joint result" that comes about — not because anyone specifically pushed for it, but rather as a result of a lot of individual associations

pursuing their own activities singlemindedly. I don't mean that we don't cooperate with each other as groups — look at our work on the Presidential Disability Amendment and with the Federal Tax Lien Task Force. But it is a gross mistake to think that the associations headquartered in Washington all have some sort of master plan by which they program their association's activities for the years to come. Nothing could be further from the truth.

We spend most of our time trying to put out brush fires and we can little afford to try to work on a long-range legislative program. We do have long-range objectives that we try to pursue over a period of time. For instance, we are trying to make the Association an organization which would concern itself more with the administration of justice, the court system, and the operations of individual bar associations and lawyers around the country. We are trying to get away from being involved in so many kinds of issues — issues that are not generic to the American Bar Association as a society of lawyers. Yet because our members will be trying cases that involve these extra-generic issues, we find ourselves frequently involved in issues that are not properly part of our concern — at least, issues which are not *our* major responsibility.[30]

Generally speaking, consensus is reached through cooperation on a regular basis between groups sharing common interests, by agreement on "who has the most right to speak" on an issue, and by conferences and summit meetings at which interested groups "thrash out" their positions and, occasionally, decide upon a leader to represent the industry position. (However, the power to speak for an industry may be immense in terms of prestige for the spokesman, provided the issue is successfully resolved; hence each group is usually sensitive about maintaining its particular group identity.)

It should be noted that cooperation on a regular basis does not necessarily produce a binding agreement between organizations, for there are two levels at which associations must operate: the pragmatic and the political — political, here, meaning intra-association politics. The pragmatic, day-to-day operations and intelligence functions of the staff of the association will sometimes conflict with the dictates of internal policy decisions or the ideas of the elected board or committee formally charged with association policy making. Thus, the staff lobbyist may know exactly how to form a working alliance with Group X, but the concessions necessary to cement the alliance may not be acceptable to higher powers in his own organization. Discussing this

---

[30] Interview with Lowell Beck, Washington, D.C., September 10, 1965.

gap between the "possible" and the "desirable," one lobbyist said, "The president of a railroad is the last guy to ask if the train is on time."

Finally, summit meetings and conferences of many organizations suffer from the same defects as the "open diplomacy" characteristic of the United Nations. Diplomacy, in the sense of discussion, agreement, and compromise, can rarely be practiced in a forum with all present to witness each compromise. It is therefore more probable that summit conferences rarely produce more than a reinforcement of existing positions and attitudes, although there is some chance that pressures from an association's friends may cause the association to modify its goal or values in accord with the conference.

6. The Greenbrier Conference and the Conference of National Organizations

Throughout America's rise to its position as a world industrial power, nagging worries have been expressed by many observers[1] that this industrial growth has been accompanied by industry control of government, that our economic or business elite has taken over major areas of public policy making and has usurped the governmental obligation to protect public interests through regulation of business and industry. Other observers,[2] less willing to accept the theory of business elite dominance, have stressed the lack of unity or cohesion within the supposed elite, the existence of cultural substructures (geographic separatism, socio-religious values, etc.) thought to be non-manipulable by any elite, multiple competing and semi-autonomous private groups and units of local and state governments, and lack of any single "dominant

---

[1] See for examples Robert A. Brady, *Business as a System of Power* (New York: Columbia University Press, 1943); Ferdinand Lundberg, *America's Sixty Families* (New York: Vanguard Press, 1937); C. Wright Mills, *The Power Elite* (New York: Oxford University Press, 1956); Floyd Hunter, *Top Leadership, U.S.A.* (Chapel Hill: University of North Carolina Press, 1959).

[2] Some representative selections are E. Pendleton Herring, *The Politics of Democracy* (New York: W. W. Norton & Co., Inc., 1940); E. E. Schattschneider, *Party Government* (New York: Farrar and Rinehart, 1942); David B. Truman, *The Governmental Process* (New York: Alfred A. Knopf, Inc., 1951); V. O. Key, *Politics, Parties, and Pressure Groups* (New York: Thomas Y. Crowell Co., 1942); Arnold M. Rose, *The Power Structure* (New York: Oxford University Press, 1967); and Robert A. Dahl, *Pluralist Democracy in the United States* (Chicago: Rand McNally & Co., 1967).

value" or "handle" by which an elite could manipulate or control a significant part of American society and government.

At one time or another within the last fifty years, almost every kind of organization has been accused of unduly influencing or overtly frustrating government policy formation. The TNEC's "classic expose"[3] distinguished between *principals* and *satellite* business groups as the major participants in the "contest for domination of public policy." Cited as principal groups were the Chamber of Commerce of the United States and the National Association of Manufacturers, the two dominant general business and industry associations, along with specific industry associations such as the Edison Electric Institute, the Association of American Railroads, the American Iron and Steel Institute, the American Petroleum Institute, the Air Transport Association, and so on. Satellite groups were defined as those "professional associations which revolve around business, largely dependent upon it for support" — the American Bankers and Investment Bankers Associations, the American Bar Association, the American Newspaper Publishers Association, etc.

Fred W. Riggs called attention to the successful operations of "catalytic groups" created on a temporary or continuing basis to draw allies together in pursuit of a common single interest, usually the passage or defeat of particular legislation. Riggs' study of the repeal of the Chinese exclusion policy[4] is paralleled by more recent examinations of catalytic groups or "peak associations" involved in liberalizing American foreign trade policy.[5]

In contrast to the single interest catalytic group is the pro-business, research-oriented Committee for Economic Development, a "business-academic partnership [which] endeavors to develop policy statements and other research products that commend themselves as guides to public and business policy . . . [in order to enable] businessmen to demonstrate constructively their concern for the general welfare . . . to earn and maintain the national and community respect essential to the successful functioning of the free enterprise capitalist system."[6] Floyd Hunter labeled this research and propaganda arm of business a good

---

[3] Temporary National Economic Committee, *Investigation of Concentration of Economic Power: Economic Power and Political Pressures* [Monograph No. 26], 76th Cong., 3rd Sess. (1941), esp. pp. 1-19, 45-56.

[4] *Pressures on Congress, A Study of the Repeal of Chinese Exclusion* (New York: King's Crown Press, 1950).

[5] Congressional Quarterly Service, *Legislators and the Lobbyists* (Washington, D.C.: Congressional Quarterly Service, 1965), pp. 61-64.

[6] Committee for Economic Development, *A Fiscal Program for a Balanced Federalism* (New York: Committee for Economic Development, 1967), back cover.

starting point "for anyone interested in a quick and partial rundown of national leadership . . . (one of the) top groupings of national leadership." [7]

Federations and unitary organizations representing general group interests have also been accused of subverting the policy formation process. Labor's AFL-CIO, agriculture's American Farm Bureau Federation, industry's National Association of Manufacturers have been cited as instrumental in blurring the line between influencing public policy and controlling public policy and as being sufficiently powerful to escape accountability to public control.

A fifth type of group, the "conference association," has been able to flourish in near obscurity. With the exception of investigations of the Business Advisory Council (now the Business Council) and other quasi-official advisory committees,[8] little attention has been paid to the "consensus-developing," "briefing," conference organization. Conferences of this type are generally distinguishable by (a) secrecy of their meetings and/or reports, (b) briefings on "confidential advance economic information" (McConnell) given them by high government officials, (c) references repeatedly made by member groups as to the "representative" quality of the conference, (d) absence at the conference of any group known to be inimical to other member groups.

In essence, the conference association is a "summit meeting" of all the foregoing types of groups — single industry and professional associations, issue oriented catalytic groups, and general interest business, industry, and professional federations and unitary organizations. The conference generally limits its activities to conducting the conference itself; that is, it does not take action as a conference but rather tries to reach a consensus concerning what actions are feasible and desirable if individual member groups wish to act *as individual groups*.

Two summit conferences of this type, almost completely unknown to press or public, are the Greenbrier Conference and the Conference of National Organizations. These associations will now be examined by analyzing their motives for cooperation, organizational structure, staff and operating procedures, and methods employed in attempting to establish conference consensus.

---

[7] *Top Leadership, U.S.A.* (Chapel Hill: University of North Carolina Press, 1959), p. 33.

[8] See Grant McConnell, *Private Power and American Democracy* (New York: Alfred A. Knopf, 1966), pp. 246-97; also U. S. House of Representatives, Antitrust Subcommittee of the Committee on the Judiciary, *WOCs and Government Advisory Groups* [*Hearings* and *Interim Report*], 84th Cong., 2nd Sess. (1956); same committee, *Interim Report on the Business Advisory Council*, 84th Cong., 1st Sess. (1955).

THE GREENBRIER CONFERENCE

In 1956, a published reference to the Greenbrier Conference (hereinafter, Greenbrier) appeared in a study of the decision-makers of American farm policy.[1] Because there are few published references to the Greenbrier, (also, McCune's book is out of print) this account of its formative period is quoted at length:

On a personal basis, it began when Charles Dana Bennett introduced to several farm leaders Thomas M. Brennan, an NAM official who was then Vice President in charge of inter-association relations . . . .

In the Spring of 1951, this group of official acquaintances and personal friends travelled to Philadelphia, to escape the Washington press corps, and formalized the joint attack on government inflation controls. They were accompanied by Braun and Co., the advertising and public relations agency of Safeway Stores, which thereafter established and staffed an off-the-record office in Philadelphia.

By this time, the group included Roger Fleming, of the Farm Bureau [in 1965 Secretary-Treasurer of the Farm Bureau and Director of the Washington office], who became a ringleader of it; Brennan of NAM, another ringleader; Rhea Blake, Vice President of the National Cotton Council; Homer Davison, Vice President of the American Meat Institute, and representatives of the American Medical Association, Investment Bankers Association, American Institute of Life Insurance Companies, American Retail Federation and the New York Stock Exchange.

The group met twice in Philadelphia early that year, then in October it moved to the plush country club facilities of the Greenbrier Hotel in the West Virginia mountains, where it was given its off-the-record name . . . .

A small committee was set up to steer the continuing operations which included Bennett as Chairman, Walter Garver of the Chamber of Commerce, Ed Stone of the Life Insurance Institute, Roland Jones of the Retail Federation, Murray Hanson of the Investment Bankers and Bert Howard of the American Medical Association. . . .

[L]ater the steering group was shuffled to include Dr. Blessingame, of the American Medical Association, as Chairman; Charles Shuman, President of the Farm Bureau; and a Vice President of Safeway.

Meetings of the full "conference" were continued on an annual basis, customarily starting on a Friday and going through the weekend. An agenda was drawn up in advance to give organizations a

---

[1] Wesley McCune, *Who's Behind Our Farm Policy?* (New York: Frederick A. Praeger, Inc., 1956), pp. 94-96.

chance to enlist support from fellow participants on policies and problems. Brennan took responsibility for the physical arrangements, but each participant paid his own way.

With the NAM furnishing the scratcher, more than a dozen powerful organizations have thus been able to scratch each other's backs in the rural atmosphere of the Greenbrier [since 1951].

James Deakin, in his book, places slightly different emphasis upon the Greenbrier Conference:

To work out the broad outlines of Chamber-NAM-Farm Bureau-AMA legislative strategy, a summit meeting is held each year at the plush Greenbrier Hotel in the West Virginia mountains. The Greenbrier Conference, as it is called, brings together the top officials of these four organizations and other sympathetic groups for three days of legislative discussions. The meeting is highly secret. Reporters are barred [and few of them know about the conference anyway, since it is never advertised].[2]

An influential national association leader commented, "The Greenbrier Conference primarily represents a common position in advance of the annual meeting. That is, the Greenbrier is composed of known conservative organizations like the Bar Association, the AMA, the Chamber of Commerce, the realtors, etc. At these meetings, the general format is for the members to be addressed or to listen to a panel discussion of eminent issues — issues currently before Congress . . . The membership of the Greenbrier Conference rarely changes . . . It was originally an offshoot or creature of the NAM, but at the present time the Greenbrier is much more under the influence of the NAM than is the Conference of National Organizations."[3]

Another business group leader, a former Chamber of Commerce employee, stressed that the Greenbrier served primarily to buttress existing views of those attending, but added that "the Greenbrier is characterized by advocacy. Whoever is speaking on Topic A is definitely trying to sell a viewpoint on that topic. He's not just giving out information; he's interested in advocacy."[4]

A representative of the life insurance industry described the Green-

---

[2] James Deakin, *The Lobbyists* (Washington, D.C.: Public Affairs Press, 1966), p. 222. Words in brackets appeared in Deakin's original typescript but do not appear in the book form.

[3] Interview, Washington, D.C., July 29, 1965. Interviewee demanded anonymity since he was at that time an attendant at one of the two conferences and an officer of the other.

[4] Interview, Washington, D.C., August, 1965. Anonymity demanded since the person is a former Chamber employee.

brier in terms of disparity between groups that get "excited" and those that do not:

Well, the Greenbrier likes to think of itself as such a summit meeting. Actually, however, it is as much a debating society as anything else. Many of the groups involved share a common conservative ideological position, but they do not share a common concern about a particular issue. As a result, some of the organizations — like the Chamber of Commerce and the NAM — take a very strong position and because we do not argue with them they assume that we are in agreement with them.

Nothing could be further from the truth. We merely do not think it of any advantage to ourselves to disagree publicly. Then the leaders get all excited and say "Let's go out and do something about this!" We let them make such a remark because we know our organization is not going to get involved in such a concern as the leaders at the Greenbrier have in mind.

On the other hand, a great deal of information is exchanged at these conferences, and it gives us some idea as to what the individual organizations consider to be a primary concern of their associations. In other words, you have an idea at the end of one of these things where every group stands on major issues and which major issue will take priority with a certain group.[5]

The Greenbrier Conference has, on at least one major issue, held more than the usual annual meeting. During the Landrum-Griffin Bill controversy, the Greenbrier met in extraordinary session, apparently acting virtually as a united front. According to a person active on the business side in that labor-management struggle, "Yes, I have heard of it. They held two Greenbrier Conferences in 1958-1959 during the Landrum-Griffin fight." [6]

Business groups lobbied successfully for the Landrum-Griffin Bill. Their success is indication of the coordination these groups achieved and upon which they operated, coordination probably developed at the Greenbrier sessions. "The major organizations involved were the NAM and the Chamber of Commerce of the United States, aided by many of their state groups; the American Farm Bureau Federation; the American Retail Federation; and the little-known National Small Business Association.

---

[5] Interview, Washington, D.C., August 24, 1965. Anonymity demanded since the person is an attendant at the Greenbrier Conference.

[6] Interview with Ed Nellor, National Right to Work Committee, Washington, D.C., July 27, 1965.

"The core of their technique, as spelled out by its practitioners, was to focus on uncommitted House members, particularly those in marginal districts. There a deliberate effort was made to translate public anger at the disclosures of union corruption by the McClellan Committee into a barrage of letters urging the congressmen to vote for a tougher labor bill." [7]

The lobby's procedure, according to this report, was first to distinguish, among congressional members generally, those from marginal districts who had never voted on a labor bill. This separation process produced one hundred twenty names. The list was then refined to include only those who favored *a* bill, and to this number were added some "safe" congressmen. This left a final list of fifty-four congressmen to be contacted.

"The rallying point was a one-hour TV program portraying union hoodlums in the juke-box field, which had run in April on Circle Theater, sponsored by the Armstrong Cork Company." Once business leaders were aware that there was a professionally produced television program showing union violence, business interest groups arranged for local stations to carry summer reruns of the Circle Theater program, either as a "public service" or sponsored by local business groups. The business lobby also heavily advertised the summer showings, and almost five million mailings advertised the program and the business lobby's position.

Examination of the Greenbrier Conference's membership roster indicates why the Conference can legitimately be termed a "summit group." The following lists, extracted from 1963 and 1964 Conference programs, illustrate the stature of organizations invited: *1963:* Investment Bankers Association, Chamber of Commerce of the United States, American Bankers Association, American Meat Institute, American Retail Federation, National Association of Manufacturers, National Association of Real Estate Boards, American Medical Political Action Committee, National Restaurant Association, American Farm Bureau Federation, National Retail Merchants Association, American Bar Association and the Pharmaceutical Manufacturers Association. (Additional organizations were present but not listed.) *1964:* American Bankers Association, American Meat Institute, Chamber of Commerce of the United States, National Association of Manufacturers, American Bar Association, National Association of Real Estate Boards, National Retail

---

[7] Bernard D. Nossiter, "Labor Bill Lobby: Mood Manipulation Is Given Credit," *Washington Post,* September 10, 1959. Also reprinted in *Congressional Record,* same date, p. 17444. The account of this technique and quotations therein are drawn from Mr. Nossiter's article.

Merchants Association, American Farm Bureau Federation, and the Investment Bankers Association.

The following organizations—not listed in the 1963 program—were expected to attend in 1964: American Medical Association, National Cotton Council, American Dental Association, American Veterinary Medical Association, National Association of Wholesalers, Health Insurance Association of America, Association of American Railroads, American Textile Manufacturers Institute, American Life Convention, Life Insurance Association of America, International Association of Ice Cream Manufacturers, National Milk Producers Federation, Association of Stock Exchange Firms, American National Cattlemen's Association, Edison Electric Institute, National Screw Machine Products Association.

In 1964, emphasis of the Greenbrier Conference was upon the balance of payments problem, discussed under the following topics: "Fundamental Domestic Causes," "Common Market Impact," "Analysis of Federal Actions Designed to Deal With the Problem," "Adequacy of Various International Monetary Arrangements."

Other sessions were devoted to "The Poverty Package" (including depressed area aid, community development subsidies, and federal health care by means of social security), "Pending Tax Legislation," "Farm Legislation for 1964," "Labor Legislation," "Civil Rights Proposals — Constitutional Implications," and presentations designed to show businessmen how to be more effective in politics.

The final item on the conference agenda was a round table discussion listed as "an opportunity for all participating organizations to present for discussion any subject not on the agenda in which there is official interest . . . or to comment or expand on any subject previously discussed." This discussion period would be the logical time for advocacy and argument leading toward any consensus developing from the Conference.

The men representing participating organizations in the Greenbrier are not mere "association hacks," staff men, or men with little knowledge of "how to meet a payroll;" present at the 1963 meeting were Per Jacobsson (Chairman and Managing Director, International Monetary Fund), John Exter (Senior Vice President, First National City Bank of New York), Ralph Reid (former Assistant Director, Bureau of the Budget), H. C. Lumb (Vice President, Republic Steel Corporation), and Clarence Davis (former Secretary of the Interior). Those who attended or were expected to attend the 1964 conference included John J. Balles (Vice President, Mellon National Bank and Trust Company), Kenton R. Cravens (Chairman of the Board, Mercantile Trust Company of St. Louis), Ira T. Ellis (economist for E. I. duPont de was wanted by a wide groundswell of membership opinion. I could do it by contacting members of my association in different cities and have them urge their local chambers to adopt a resolution calling for my policy. Secondly, Chamber policy can be influenced by the key men appointed by the Chamber to its important committees. For instance, the Chamber tax committee will have a representative from a leading Washington law firm that specializes in tax problems. Everyone knows that this man will eventually determine the Chamber's tax policy, since none of the rest of the committee members are as well informed or as "influential" as is this particular representative. Thus one could say that the Chamber has at its top policy levels a way of being sure that its own board of directors' policy is presented to key Chamber committees. To this extent, the Chamber is not a completely democratic organization.

Any study of the Chamber must concentrate on the "federation aspects" of the Chamber. To the extent that the Chamber is a federation, it obviously cannot speak with a united voice, since it must represent each of its group members. The Chamber does not speak with the single voice of business; rather it adds the Chamber's weight to the voice of each individual association which belongs to the Chamber — that is, whenever the Chamber is in agreement with the position of the individual association.

I'm high on Booth [the executive vice president] as a coordinator. He has done a fantastic job over the years of getting and keeping together the dissimilar groups that make up the Chamber. He's a great coordinator. And I wouldn't have his job for anything in the world!

Interview with Mr. E.:

In my eight years with the Chamber I learned one thing that many people don't realize. Don't make the mistake of assuming that the Chamber is a monolithic organization. It has factions within it, within its staff and between the national, the state, and local chambers of commerce.

For instance, there are roughly three groups on the Chamber staff in Washington. The first is a liberal group, the second is a "swing" or "floater" group, and the third is a conservative group. It may seem odd, but the Chamber will enact liberal policies, middle of the road policies, and conservative policies. How? Primarily because — through successful management of getting proper personnel on his committees — a Chamber department manager or committee secretary can succeed in getting his own policies adopted by his committee and then sent to the board of directors for confirmation as "national" policy.

Have you noted that there is a significant absence of important or key businessmen on the Chamber of Commerce board of directors?

This occurs for two reasons. First, large corporation presidents do not wish to run against small businessmen. The corporation president might lose — and what would that do for his image? Second, large corporation presidents are not manageable by Chamber of Commerce staff members. In other words, if a department manager puts on his committee a significant or key businessman from a large corporation, the staff man will not be able to "manage" that committee member. It will be the other way around. The large dues-paying member will end up having his policy adopted with or without the consent or approval of the staff men.

The quality of research done at the Chamber has been going down steadily over the last decade. This decline is due to the fact that Booth [the executive vice president] prefers to have research done which will justify policy proposals rather than research which will illuminate a situation. In other words, if the Chamber decides it is against foreign trade, [Booth] wants research done which will justify the Chamber's position. He doesn't want general research which would indicate what position the Chamber should take on the subject of foreign trade in the first place.

As far as administration in the Chamber goes, you may have come across the time when an incoming president of the Chamber insisted that Booth bring in at the executive level two aides who would share in administrative coordination and direction of Chamber affairs internally. Booth objected but acquiesced; immediately after the president's term had ended, Booth saw to it that the two aides were discharged. One is now the executive vice president of his own chamber on the West Coast, the other is a West Coast vice president of a national life insurance company.

Interview with Mr. F:

Has anyone mentioned to you the famous floor fight at the 1962 policy luncheon?[7] That was a dilly! The floor fight destroyed any illusion of democratic decision-making within the Chamber of Commerce.

But oddly enough, that debacle did result in better and more

---

[7] "Because of the Chamber's diligent cultivation of cohesion, convention floor fights rarely break out. During the 1962 policy luncheon, however, a rank-and-file revolt succeeded in turning down the Policy Committee's recommendation opposing subsidies to industries and workers injured by tariff revisions. The revolt was apparently a manifestation of hostility to the Chamber's standing policy favoring reduction of trade barriers. Perceiving its latitude of operation in jeopardy, Chamber officers jumped in and, after three votes, obtained a reversal of the original vote. Chamber veterans said there was no precedent for the two-hour wrangle in the 50-year history of the organization." Roger Harry Davidson, "The Depressed Areas Controversy: A Study in the Politics of American Business" (Unpublished Ph.D. thesis, Columbia University, 1963), p. 222. See also *Washington Post,* May 3, 1962; *CQ Legislators and the Lobbyists, op. cit.,* p. 62.

democratic policy-making procedures. Booth began sending out letters to members informing them of what policy was being considered by the Chamber and asking them for comments. He started communicating with Chamber committee members and regular members informing them of what action had been taken by committees and calling for comments on this action from Chamber members. *Now*, Chamber policy could be turned around or reversed by a grassroots membership pressure.

The general educational level of Chamber employees — except in the legal, economics, and foreign policy departments — is too low. The middle management level is the weakest. There, morale is lousy. The number two and number three man in each department are not worth a damn. Personnel has too high a turnover; the assistant department managers are demoralized and are not contributing. I think this is because the department managers know they cannot move up to [Booth's] job and therefore they freeze everyone below them. That way nobody gets prestige, and the managers try to hog all the credit. It's what I call "psychic peonage."

All the petty politicking and gossiping and bad morale within the Chamber are due to the fact that the personnel don't know where they stand and are trying to find out through all this gossiping.

You know about the "umbrella brigade"? Booth requires staff members — some of them with Ph.D.'s — to stand by the front door with umbrellas if a shower occurs while dignitaries are arriving for a Chamber conference or meeting. That's the kind of thing he does that demeans people. They're little things, but they irritate.

In my opinion, Chamber committees could be most effective in drawing up good study papers. These could be used by the business community as well as the Chamber to firm up a consensus. Chamber committees are already effective in rendering services to members, and that's one place the Chamber earns its dues.

I do think that the Chamber is the one organization that could speak for American business.

Summary of Interviews

In general, the interviews reported above indicate that former staff members believe several areas of national Chamber internal operations could be improved.

First, "the board of directors lacks key business leaders whose weight would be felt both within the Chamber and within the general business community." This criticism overlooks the fact that there are leading business figures on the Chamber's board. In 1964, Robert S. Ingersoll (Chairman and Chief Executive Officer, Borg-Warner Corporation), Louis B. Lundbord (Executive Vice President, Bank of America), Erwin D. Canham (Editor in Chief, *Christian Science Mon-*

itor), Carl J. Gilbert (Chairman of the Board, The Gillette Company), Frank A. Kemp (President, Great Western Sugar Company), and L. B. Worthington (President, United States Steel Company) were members of the board of directors.

It is questionable whether such men could be "managed" by Booth, the executive vice president, or by other staff members. What apparently irks the Chamber staff and former employees is that few men of stature or reputation *actively serve* on the board. In many organizations, members of boards of directors are often appointed or elected for their prestige, with the understanding that "only a few days of their time" will be required during the year. Some members of the Chamber's board probably are in this category, if informal remarks of Chamber employees are considered valid.

Few of those interviewed asserted or implied that the board could be "managed" by the executive vice president or other staff members. Most agreed that the executive vice president did not have "control" of the board and that the Chamber was not "run by its staff."

There was general agreement that the educational level of the Chamber staff was lower than one would expect in one of the nation's leading business organizations. Personnel records from the Chamber of Commerce could disprove this, but these records are not generally available. It appears, however, that most staff members have been graduated from college but the majority have little or no graduate training.

There is virtually unanimous agreement among former employees interviewed that the Chamber's middle management level needs reorganization and the infusion of new personnel. In the Chamber's staff organization, the "middle management" level includes departmental assistants and managers of the lesser departments. Many complaints were directed at the gap between department managers and the executive vice president. This breach was expressed as a gap in "human relations" and as a breakdown of internal communications between department managers and the executive vice president—a breakdown caused by (1) "jumping of the chain of command" by employees below the department manager level (they were free to bypass department managers and go to the top); and (2) the barrier imposed by the five "group managers" or "general managers" who coordinate workings of departments under their jurisdiction (these coordinators were said to be, in effect, poor advocates of the department managers).

There was unanimous agreement by these former employees that the quality of Chamber research should be greatly improved. The existing attitude and performance of researchers were criticized on the grounds that they were biased toward policy positions already adopted and that research was often no more than publicity-grinding for a viewpoint a Chamber member wished to justify.

Finally, there were several severe comments criticizing the lack of internal democracy within the Chamber. "Committee stacking," "veneer of democracy overlaying a rigid authoritarian structure," "lacks real democracy," "illusion of democratic decision-making" were some of the more temperate criticisms.

As expressed in an earlier chapter, perhaps one should not expect to find much "internal democracy" within such an organization as the Chamber, unless one considers the relations between decision-makers *on the same level* or the procedures governing relations between members and the organizational staff. The interviews quoted illustrate that there *is* "a good competitive system" between department managers and "managers have lots of freedom to run their own departments." This appears to indicate that there is "rough" equality or democracy among the department managers. In short, complaints regarding internal democracy actually relate to the discrepancy between the *procedural forms* by which policy is supposed to be made (by committees, board of directors, and the annual meeting) and the alleged practice of policy making by "blue chip" companies and clever staff members who can "manage" their committees.

At least one criticism made by former employees appears to be valid: the Chamber does not in fact operate with the "real democracy" it professes. But, as virtually all organizational studies indicate, few large organizations operate in a "really democratic" fashion. The Chamber is no exception to this general rule and merits no individual criticism for following what appears to be a general custom of organizational behavior.

One further interview should be reported. A nationally-known, Washington-based reporter was asked for opinions of the Chamber of Commerce's internal organization, opinions reached after several years of covering Chamber functions, press conferences, and annual meetings. He said, "That's the damnedest organization I ever saw. You know, it's almost sovietized. It's stratified rigidly; the employees—even department managers—have to fill out little pink slips if they're even five minutes late to work. That's a real orphan organization, a neglected group that really ought to be studied by somebody from the inside."

THE CHAMBER OF COMMERCE IN MOTION

In any structure, an "action" section has to put the policy stands to work. The Chamber of Commerce is structured to embody this basic premise.

The Legislative Department

In July, 1965, the Chamber's Legislative Department staff consisted of about twelve people including Theron J. Rice, legislative general manager; Don Goodall, legislative director and assistant manager; Donald Young, assistant; Francis M. Judge, Senate reporter; John McLees, House reporter; Charles Armentrout, editor of "Congressional Action"; John W. Davies, editor of "Here's the Issue"; Spencer Johnson, coordinator of Congressional Action Committee Services; and secretarial employees.[8] As far as can be determined, only Rice, Goodall, and Johnson were registered lobbyists.

Functions and purposes of the Legislative Department are to collect and disseminate legislative information, to coordinate all Chamber legislative work (including lobbying), to assist association members in forming Congressional Action Committees to study pending legislation, to provide Chamber members with specific information regarding specific bills and their status in Congress, to oversee all communications between the national Chamber and Congress to prevent "a communications glut," to "supervise the final polishing of testimony for presentation before Congressional committees . . . and to counsel with the Chamber's policy departments concerning legislative strategy."

To coordinate lobbying assignments and ensure that every department manager is aware of work underway on legislative interests, each department completes an "Issue Strategy Checklist" identifying issues on which it is currently working. Copies of these checklists are then sent to all departments concerned with legislative affairs to enable each department to know what every other department is doing.

The following questions from the Strategy Checklist indicate the thoroughness with which the Chamber prepares a legislative campaign:

Department responsible?

Other departments interested?

Has policy been checked with policy committee secretary?

Any policy problems? If so, action proposed?

Action pending in which house before which committee?

Bill proponents?

Bill opponents?

---

[8] This description of the personnel, purposes, and functions of the national Chamber is taken from "Association Letter" (Washington, D.C.: CCUS, [July] 1965), p. 3.

Most influential members of the Committee of jurisdiction and their stand on this issue?

"Swing" members of Committee of jurisdiction?

Indicate 1st, 2nd, 3rd choice of objectives re this bill: Pass, Kill, Amend, Recommit, Delay, Other

Presentation (if any) will be in form of: Testimony, statement, or letter (Indicate)

Witness prospect list (Name and Organization)

Any major segment of membership unhappy with our position? If yes, who?

List major arguments we must counter

What is our proposed solution?

List associations, member companies and other groups vitally interested in this issue

Of the above groups, which have particular influence with the Congressmen shown who will play a leadership role in determining the outcome of this issue? (Give name of group and congressmen-leaders)

After completing this much of the Issue Strategy Checklist, the department then indicates what action it proposes and what utilization of Chamber resources are contemplated. Blanks are provided for the department to indicate anticipated use of Chamber personnel, meetings, and communications media. One section of the checklist calls for the department to indicate its intentions regarding "organizing external support." Under this section are listed the kinds of external support that *may* be available to the Chamber:

State chambers

Local chamber Congressional Action Committees

Associations

(a) Association breakfast group

(b) Special trade groups

(c) *Greenbrier group and/or conference**

Washington Reps [Representatives of major companies]

Public affairs executives

*Special Strategy group**

[*Emphasis supplied]

ist" position and a "states rights" position advocated by people like the NRMA, the credit retailers would probably choose the federalist position, simply because they would prefer not to be associated with a position that is made too politically extreme by propaganda.[7]

A spokesman for the American Bankers Association (hereafter ABA) did not agree with all the content of the interview quoted above. According to this ABA spokesman: [8]

The ABA established their policy toward the Douglas Credit Bill as early as 1960. The ABA generally supports full disclosure of interest rates to consumers but objects specifically to the "annual rate" requirements on the grounds that (1) it would be impossible to figure annual rates because there were too many variables in the equation, (2) this area of regulation of consumer credit should be left to the states, not the federal government, and (3) the approach taken by Senator Douglas appears to be an obvious attempt to introduce control of credit rates, not merely requiring interest rate disclosure.

In 1964, the Commission on Uniform State Laws got in touch with the ABA on its own initiative. The Commission had studied the question of consumer credit laws in the 1950's and had wanted to draft a uniform credit law. They discontinued their study until 1964 because they felt the field was too complicated. Then in 1964 they contacted the American Bar Association to find out what their position would be on a uniform credit law. The Bar wholeheartedly welcomed the idea of a nationwide study of credit policy under the auspices of the Commission. The ABA felt, and still feels, that such a study would be the best solution to the problem of interest rate disclosure and general credit legislation, rather than have a study directed by a senate investigating committee or a single senator.

The ABA agreed to put in one-half ($50,000) of the operating budget for the Commission study group for the first year, provided the Commission then raised a like amount from all other segments of the commercial finance industry. The study had one simple goal — the feasibility of a uniform consumer credit law — and it has taken 13 months to come up with the first suggestions. The Commission feels that such a law is feasible and that a model law should be ready for introduction to state legislatures as early as 1967 or 1968.

---

[7] This lengthy interview was given to the author over a period of several days in August 1965. In view of the close correspondence in language and content between the Duscha article and this interview, it is possible that Duscha received much of his information from this Senate source — or vice versa.

[8] Anonymity granted by request; the spokesman was, in 1965, in the office of the Federal Administrative Counsel, American Bankers Association, Washington, D.C.

The ABA spokesman was then asked to comment on a report that the financial industry's position was formulated by the small loan companies who then withdrew, leaving the National Retail Merchants and the Federated Department Stores to direct the fight. Said the ABA spokesman, "Yours is a very good surmise," but provided no additional information.

The ABA led the fight against the early Douglas bills in at least one respect, as the chief financial sponsor of the study made by the Commission on Uniform State Laws. In other words, the ABA asserted its leadership by supporting the major alternative to federal regulation of consumer credit practices.

The ABA spokesman did not agree with the Senate source's description of small banks' influence on larger banking and credit institutions:

The American Bankers Association's administrative committee is the chief policy-making and policy approval organ within the ABA. This is a balanced committee. Both small and large banks and various types of banking institutions are fairly represented. I don't feel that the conservatism of small banks overly influences the policy of the ABA. Nor do I think that the small credit dispensers can hold a particular club over the bankers' heads. I have not run into this in any case I can think of. I don't know of any "trade-out" between the small credit dispensers on the local level and the national bankers on the other.

Note that the American Bankers Association was not at that time a member of the national Chamber, although there was close cooperation between the two groups in opposing truth in lending. As was observed in an earlier quotation, Edwin J. Frey, a Grand Rapids banker, was a member of the Chamber's board of directors and "had been active within both the Chamber and the ABA in advising a stand against the Douglas Bill."

In 1965, Archie K. Davis, an ABA vice-president,[9] was a member of the Chamber's Finance Committee,[10] not in his capacity as an officer of the ABA, of course, but as chairman of the board of the Wachovia Bank and Trust Company, Winston-Salem, North Carolina (a bank maintaining membership in a state or local Chamber of Commerce or other association that was a member of the national Chamber). Thus,

---

[9] "Washington Bulletin" (Washington, D.C.: ABA, May 5, 1965 [General Bulletin No. 4-65]), p. 1.
[10] *Officers, Directors, and Committeemen 1964–1965* (Washington, D.C.: Chamber of Commerce of the United States, 1964), p. 24. Hereafter the national Chamber will be cited as CCUS.

although the national Chamber declares that it works only with its association or business members, it is obvious that intergroup cooperation between the ABA and the Chamber was, at that time, established and active.

Intergroup Lobbying and Cooperation: The Proponents

Major forces supporting truth in lending included, prior to 1966, the AFL-CIO, Credit Union National Association, the President's Consumer Advisory Council, National Consumers League, and various associations of retired persons, garden clubs, and consumers' cooperatives, including the Consumers Union and the Cooperative League of the USA. As Julius Duscha reported:

> Organizations favoring the bill include the AFL-CIO and the Credit Union National Association as well as some mutual savings banks and well-meaning but anemic consumers' groups. This support has been far from sturdy. Nowadays, the AFL-CIO has plenty of troubles getting its way with labor legislation, and its influence on issues like consumer credit is marginal. Nor are the credit unions any match for finance companies and banks.[11]

A National Retail Merchants Association spokesman also said that credit unions were the Douglas Bill's chief supporters "but we can't prove it." In addition, a confidential memorandum from a major national professional association reported to members of one of its legislative committees:[12]

> What is really behind this bill? It is apparent that the credit union movement instigated this legislation. Credit unions are pushing actively for it now. If it is passed there is a strong possibility that credit unions will actually obtain a near monopoly in consumer lending. They will be able to advertise for rates far less than the average retail lender, even though the comparison would be unfair. An interesting fact to note is the very close tie between labor unions and credit unions. The result of passage of legislation embodying the simple annual rate would mean enormous profits to credit unions and, in turn [to] labor groups which provide for a great bulk of credit union financing. Credit unions are presently holding a distinct advantage over all other lenders in that there are no taxes on their profits.

There is speculation that credit unions are making plans to expand

---

[11] Duscha, *op. cit.*, p. 77.

[12] The memorandum was made available to the author with the provision that sufficient editing would be done to disguise the name of the association and its field.

their operations into the mortgage field, lending money to those other than members. There is also speculation that the entire scope of credit union activity will be broadened . . . .

In other words, there is much more behind the Douglas Bill then [*sic*] simply an effort to protect the unknowing consumer. Therefore rumblings are present for a possible investigation of credit union activity — perhaps even resulting in a bill introduced to tax their profits. This is only talk but could divert the credit unions from pushing for such measures as the Douglas Bill. Without the credit unions urging it, the thrust for it would lose most of its steam.

Alliance Among the Proponents: The Consumer Assembly

Although the writer of the above memorandum may have been correct in his belief that credit unions were active in support of truth in lending legislation, it is also apparent that advancement of consumer interests is becoming increasingly popular as a political issue upon which liberal candidates can campaign.

The federal government gave its approval to "consumerism" in 1962 by establishing the Consumer Advisory Council. Under the initial leadership of Esther Peterson, former Assistant Secretary of Labor, the Council was active that year and later in proposing truth in lending and truth in packaging measures to protect consumers against alleged fraud and misrepresentation in the marketplace. Again, in 1967-68, these measures gained additional prestige through the direct interest of President Johnson.

Pressures on Congress for consumer legislation increased markedly after a 1966 conference of interested groups. On April 25-27, in Washington, D.C., the "Consumer Assembly 1966" convened to make public the growing demand for such protective legislation as truth in lending and packaging. Stressing their broad agreement on the need for such protection, the following groups urged Congress to react appropriately—or reap the consequences at the polls: AFL-CIO (and associated organizations and member groups), American Association of Retired Persons, American Public Power Association, American Veterans Committee, Consumers Union, National Consumers League, Cooperative League of the U.S. (and other cooperative groups), Council on Consumer Information, CUNA International, General Federation of Women's Clubs, National Association for the Advancement of Colored People, National Farmers Union, plus Catholic and other church groups.

Effects of the Consumer Assembly cannot be measured directly, although it is reasonable to state that the Assembly increased the pressures on Congress to enact consumer legislation. For example, Assembly delegates were instructed in how to make efficient requests to their own congressmen. Congressmen shortly thereafter reported increases in the number of communications received favoring consumer legislation. Finally, without attempting to prove a cause and effect relationship, it is logical to relate the formation of the Assembly with the passage in late November 1966 of the truth in packaging bill (PL 89-755) and later the truth in lending bill (PL 90-321) in May 1968.

Congressional-Interest Group Cooperation

Cooperation between friendly congressmen and interest groups obviously is important in the success of legislative efforts. Ability to count the votes in committees and subcommittees frequently depends upon information provided for groups by members of congressional committees. The following quotations, from the confidential memorandum cited earlier, are ample illustration:

On [°] I attended a small meeting of individuals who have positions against S. 750, the Douglas Credit Disclosure Bill. Senator Bennett [R.-Utah] was present and gave us his first hand knowledge as to the present status of the bill and the outlook for the immediate future . . . .
Senator Douglas possibly will present at least two variations over past bills . . . Senator Bennett sees nothing in these two possible variations which would make the bill more palatable.
Senator Robertson [D-Va.], Chairman of the Full Senate Banking Committee, has stated that he does not intend to call hearings until it is perfectly convenient to all concerned. In other words, he is in no hurry. Hearings probably will be held, but later in the session. It is positive that Senator Robertson and the Republican Senators Bennett, Simpson and Dominick, will oppose it in subcommittee. The opposition must have one more man to keep the bill from going to the full committee. The swing man is Senator Muskie. Last year he did not vote; however his presence and vote would have made no difference since five votes were needed to recommend the bill to the full committee.
Senator Long of Missouri, who is firmly against the legislation, reports that unless Douglas makes some changes Senator Muskie probably will not support it. The big question now — will the variations, as stated above, be enough to allow Senator Muskie to support it?
If the bill goes to the full Committee then what? The opposition has five sure votes on the full Banking Committee, including

---

*Date deleted to ensure anonymity.

Senator Long of Missouri. The outcome in the full Committee will hinge upon Senators McIntyre [D.-N.H.], Javits and Sparkman. Senator McIntyre probably will follow Muskie. Of course, he realizes that he must be fairly conservative due to his constituency. Senator Javits is in favor of the principle of the bill, but not the simple annual rate. He will support it if it is brought more into line with the law in New York. As to Senator Sparkman, if the President *really* wants it he will support it. However, if there is no strong pressure from the White House, he probably will not. In that connection, there is some speculation, according to this morning's *Washington Post*, that White House aides have urged the soft pedaling of consumer programs as part of efforts to restore business confidence in the Administration....

If it gets to the House, it will pass right through. Whereas Senator Robertson is not the "boss" of his committee, Rep. Wright Patman [D-Tex.] is in control of House Banking. Rep. Patman has not committed himself on the bill [;] however he is a friend of Douglas.

But the House will not act in any way until Douglas has been successful on the Senate side. This is Douglas' show entirely, and nobody will attempt to steal it from him.

Senator Muskie, therefore, seems to be the key to enactment. It appears that if the bill leaves the subcommittee, it will become law — *with a simple annual rate provision*.... [Emphasis is original.]

These quotations from an interest group memorandum illustrate several points: First, interest groups, with the assistance of friendly congressmen, are willing to consider utilizing a senate investigating committee as a diversionary tactic to place the opposition in an off-balance position to prevent its giving full strength to a controversy. Second, potential White House influence is clearly stated. Senator Sparkman is described as willing to oppose the S.750 bill if he received no strong pressure from the White House, but as willing to support the President if the President really urged him.

Third, the committee chairman obviously has a powerful role not at all dependent on party ties. Senator Robertson, a Democrat, is described as willing to stall committee hearings although the subcommittee chairman, Senator Douglas (another Democrat), is anxious for hearings to begin. (Robertson consistently voted with the Republicans, both in subcommittee and full committee.)

Fourth, it is clear that a truth in lending bill was expected to have full House support, if the bill moved that far. Not stated, but fully known by the interest group preparing the memorandum, was the probability that such a bill would have little difficulty in the Senate if it could be dislodged from the Senate Banking and Currency Committee —even without a favorable report, according to some sources.

These facts illustrate interest groups' success in blocking legislation which would have a clear majority of congressional support, and that the most successful method of blocking such legislation is to make certain that the bill does not leave the subcommittee to which it is assigned.

The previous quotations illustrating intergroup lobbying on the Douglas Bill in its various forms do not indicate the large number of powerful associations and companies opposing such legislation.

The scope and mass of opposition is more apparent in the following partial list [13] of witnesses who at some time testified against truth in lending bills: American Retail Federation, National Automobile Dealers Association, National Association of Retail Clothiers and Furnishers, National Retail Merchants Association, Montgomery Ward & Company, Sears Roebuck & Company, American Bankers Association (and five other bank associations), C.I.T. Financial Corporation, General Motors Acceptance Corporation, John Hancock Life Insurance Company, New York Stock Exchange and Boston Stock Exchange, National Association of Manufacturers, National Small Business Association, Chamber of Commerce of the United States, American Bar Association, National Conference of Commissioners on Uniform State Laws (cited in the text as Commission on Uniform State Laws), National Consumer Finance Association (and six state finance associations), and the National Association of Better Business Bureaus, Inc.

This description of intergroup lobbying concerning credit disclosure bills, has, thus far, paid little attention to issues and arguments involved. There were reasonable arguments on both sides. Proponents said such legislation would provide full credit information disclosure, prohibiting hidden and excessive credit charges, allowing the consumer to shop for the least expensive and most suitable credit arrangement. The proponents also argued that the states were apparently unwilling to act in this field.

Opponents argued in part that it was mathematically impossible to compute a "simple annual rate" on many kinds of credit transactions, especially on a "revolving credit" charge account. In addition, opponents argued that merchants would merely include (or bury) credit costs in prices, thus concealing even more credit information from consumers. Finally, they proclaimed that legislation of this kind was so complex and far reaching that a new federal bureaucracy would be needed—one whose role would soon expand into actual *control* of credit *and* prices. The opponents prophesied the "destruction of capital-

---

[13] From *The Truth About "Truth-in-Lending" Legislation* (Washington, D.C.: National Small Business Association, 1965), pp. 15-17.

ism," the creation of even more federal controls, and further threats to states' rights and power—all politically inflammatory visions.

In this particular issue, the national Chamber of Commerce did not play a commanding role, yet it performed the function of which it is most proud: providing a forum in which interested Chamber members could discuss, argue, and attempt to reach consensus regarding adoption of "the position for business" generally and the Chamber in particular. The Chamber's policy manual provided any authorization necessary for Chamber activity against these bills: "Authority for the Chamber's opposition was *reaffirmed* as recently as May 2 [1962] by the voting delegates of the Chamber's organization members, assembled in policy session during the Chamber's 50th annual meeting." [14]

In addition, the Chamber worked diligently to muster support for senators backing the Chamber's position in subcommittee and full committee meetings and hearings. The manager of the Manufacture-Distribution Department, in a letter to Chamber of Commerce executives working with Congressional Action Committees,[15] wrote:

Because the [Douglas] bill obviously now has Administration backing, this magnifies the problem of heading off the legislation. As in the past, though, our best opportunity to do this is still within the subcommittee itself. Fortunately, five of the ten members of the subcommittee still share our views about the bill — and so long as they are opposed to it, Senator Douglas cannot muster a majority vote for reporting his bill . . . .

Unfortunately, these five men are receiving little, if any, mail about this issue from businessmen and business organizations. This is a bad situation. It's difficult enough for a politician to stand against a bill such as this which has "truth in lending" as its publicized objective . . . If we don't soften the difficulty with our own letters of appreciation and encouragement, we really will have no one to blame but ourselves if we wake up some morning and find that this five-vote bloc has disappeared.

What I'm requesting, therefore, is quite obvious. Will you have at least two or three of your Committee members write a letter to these five Senators, expressing appreciation for their position on S. 1740 and encouraging them to continue standing fast. It would be appropriate to say a little something "extra" in your letter to Senator Bennett,

---

[14] Statement of Joseph N. Anderson (representing the national Chamber of Commerce), U.S. Senate, Subcommittee of the Committee on Banking and Currency, *Hearings: Truth in Lending—1962*, 87th Cong., 2nd Sess. (May 8-18, 1962), p. 276. Emphasis added. (See also *Policy Declarations 1964–1965* [Washington, D.C.: CCUS, 1964], p. 11.)

[15] *Ibid.*, pp. 317-18.

for he has been our most outstanding spokesman — not just this year, but also in 1960 and 1961 . . . .

Here are the five Senators who ought to know of our gratitude:

Wallace F. Bennett	(of Utah)
Homer E. Capehart	(of Indiana)
Prescott Bush	(of Connecticut)
J. Glenn Beall	(of Maryland)
A. Willis Robertson	(of Virginia)

I'd appreciate a copy of any letters your members write — and it wouldn't be a bad idea for copies to be sent to your own senators.

Summary: Truth in Lending

Prior to the 1966 congressional elections, the sides had been so steadfastly drawn that all Senate truth in lending bills met the fate their first proponent forecast: they would not be passed during his political lifetime. But the Senate of the 90th Congress, First Session, passed S.5, a Douglas-type truth in lending bill, by a 92-0 roll call vote. What happened to produce such dramatic change in the Senate's attitude toward truth in lending legislation?

First, President Johnson made a strong bid for passage of the bill during the First and Second Sessions—in contrast to weaker presidential efforts in previous years when passage was believed likely to alienate the business community from the Great Society.

Second, several compromises were arranged to soften bill provisions found to be most objectionable to the credit industry and department stores. Lenders were allowed an option to inform consumers of an "average effective annual rate" (what the lender expected to earn from credit transactions) which would normally be less than the other two rates the lender was required to state. Further, until January 1, 1971, lenders could state their charges in dollars per hundred. As another compromise, the conference report set the definition of an "extortionate" rate of interest at forty-five percent, a figure so high as to not disturb any legitimate creditor.

Third, Federated Department Stores (reportedly the strategist for the National Retail Merchants Association's opposition) softened its opposition, now insisting only that no blanket annual rate or ceiling be set on revolving charge accounts.

Fourth, the 1966 elections produced some notable changes in the battle order. Gone from the full committee chair was Willis Robertson, an implacable foe of truth in lending, and Strom Thurmond, another vigorous opponent. New additions to the committee included Brooke of

Maryland—a young and somewhat aggressive senator—provided the impetus. We had a strong fifteen-man group. We could make long speeches to keep things going on the floor. We also knew where the bodies were buried and how to hold the opposition's feet to the fire." [52]

The Dirksen Amendment in Review

Controversy on the Dirksen Amendment continued into the 89th Congress's second session, giving every indication that it would not be resolved easily. Both sides chose to work through large coalitions— probably the only method by which the necessary popular support and financing could be organized to sustain a long campaign. Proponents of the amendment employed a highly-skilled public relations firm to provide day-to-day direction of their efforts; opponents depended upon coordinated leadership through union affiliations with civil rights groups, and upon the leadership of key senators opposed to the amendment.

Regardless of the issue's merit, it is obvious that reapportionment is the kind of issue about which individuals and groups become emotionally aroused, willing to participate personally and financially.

Groups with rural interests feared they had much to lose—and with reason: they had jealously guarded those interests for a hundred years! Many people involved with the opposition said, in essence, "If the rural interests hadn't been so stingy for so long, they wouldn't be in the position of losing it all at once, as they are now."

Urban interests, on the other hand, felt they had been dominated too long by cows and trees and fence posts: they wanted representation *now* and appeared willing to settle for no less than apportionment based on population.

(It would be interesting to know how the apportionment picture will look in fifty years. Will the population have returned to the rural areas and will the cities and suburbs then be cut off short as the rural areas are today? Will the rural areas then be any less vengeful than the urban interests today?)

Lobbying concerning the Dirksen Amendment is an example of the tangled web of influence and pressure that is so difficult to unravel in documenting intergroup cooperation. The separate activities of the different groups composing the proponents and opponents can be isolated and discussed, but the question remains, "How and to what degree were activities of each side coordinated?" From the facts known, it is possible to infer that Ernest Tupper or Clem Whitaker *could* answer

---

[52] Interview with Senator Joseph S. Clark, Washington, D.C., August 10, 1965.

that question. Senator Dirksen or one of his staff also might hold the answer. But the fact is that—like good magicians—the principals in this controversy are unwilling to show how their tricks are performed. Thus, one can say "these facts are proven," "these events occurred," and "these were the principal actors"; but the intergroup cooperation must be inferred—until such time as one of the leaders breaks his silence. And, as long as any hope exists that the Dirksen Amendment might be adopted, none of these principal performers will speak off-stage.

Part 4
A Look Ahead

9.   Boundaries of Interest Group Activities

Limitation by Legal Controls: The Lobbying Act of 1946

The Lobbying Act was enacted as Title III of the Legislative Reorganization Act of 1946. In brief, the Lobbying Act has two requirements: (1) Any person hired by someone else for the principal purpose of lobbying Congress is required to register with the Secretary of the Senate and the Clerk of the House and file quarterly financial reports concerning income, activities and expenses. (2) Organizations receiving and spending money for the *principal* purpose of influencing legislation do not necessarily have to register, but are required to file quarterly spending reports concerning their attempts to influence legislation.

In *U.S. vs. Harriss,*[1] the United States Supreme Court limited the scope of the Lobbying Act. According to the language and subsequent interpretation of the Court's ruling, (1) persons or groups spending their own funds (and not soliciting or collecting funds for the purpose of influencing legislation) were not covered by the Act; (2) organizations whose *principal* purpose was not the influencing of legislation were not covered by the Act—regardless of what activities they carried on; (3) unless the organization carried on or contemplated *direct* contact with members of Congress, for the purpose of influencing legislation, the organization was not covered by the Act.

Thus the Lobbying Act, as modified by the *Harriss* decision, dis-

---

[1] 347 U.S. 612.

tinguishes between the person or group hired as a lobbyist for pay by someone else, and the group lobbying only for itself (its own members) and not for hire as a lobbyist by another party. The first group must register under the Act and file quarterly reports; the second group need not register (although many do) but must file quarterly reports. Furthermore, the second group may refuse to register on the grounds that (a) its principal purpose is not the influencing of legislation, or (b) its lobbying activities are of the grassroots variety only and do not involve direct contacts with members of Congress, or (c) both of these.

Among the national groups which have not filed reports for most years, according to Larry King,[2] are the American Bankers Association, the National Association of Manufacturers, the American Public Power Association, and some of the largest defense contractors (who maintain "more Washington suites than Alabama has outside agitators"). The Chamber of Commerce of the United States also refused at one point to report any spending as an organization under the act.[3]

Since its enactment in 1946, the Lobbying Act has exhibited certain deficiencies making it somewhat less than fully effective as a means of regulating interest group activities by publicizing their finances and interests. As summarized by George Galloway, these deficiencies exist with respect to (1) coverage, (2) information required, (3) publicity given, (4) administration, and (5) enforcement.[4]

Senator William Proxmire (D-Wis.) termed the Lobbying Act "a farce," saying, "We made a study recently of some forty-one lobbyists . . . who did file, and we found that three-quarters of these . . . didn't comply with the law after they had filed. They failed to state from where the money came that paid them; they failed to state what particular bill they were interested in; and on the basis of this study, which I think is fairly typical, it's clear that even those who do file their reports —and I'm sure that most do not—the compliance means very, very little. . . ." [5]

If the Lobbying Act is "a farce," two courses seem to be open to Congress: either amend it, or achieve its ostensible purpose by another means.

There have been consistent attempts to amend the Act, including legislation introduced in the 90th Congress. Bills have been introduced

---

[2] "Washington's Money Birds," *Harper's Magazine,* Vol. CCXXXI, No.1383 (August, 1965), p. 45.

[3] Congressional Quarterly Service, *Legislators and the Lobbyists,* (Washington. D.C.: Congressional Quarterly Service, 1965), p. 53. Hereafter cited as *CQ.*

[4] U.S. Senate, Special Committee to Investigate Political Activities, Lobbying, and Campaign Contributions, *Final Report,* 85th Cong., 1st Sess. (May 31, 1957), p. 196.

[5] June 27, 1964 television broadcast, reported by *CQ, op. cit.,* p. 54.

"for nineteen consecutive years to make the law more meaningful [but] they have quietly withered on the vine. 'Nobody,' says Congressman Morris Udall, Arizona Democrat, 'is lobbying for them.' " [6]

Congress might also attempt to achieve the Act's purposes by other means. The policy and operations of the Internal Revenue Service (IRS) have been such as to impose a genuine limit on interest groups' activities. Present IRS regulations clearly stipulate that expenses for propaganda or lobbying concerning legislation are not deductible if the persuasive material is directed at the general public, although the same expenses are deductible if the material is directed solely at the organization's members or at Congress (provided the bill being lobbied would affect the "direct interest" of the organization's members). Activities which do not meet these criteria, or which are of such amount or extent as to stamp the organization as "principally" devoting its time to lobbying, may provoke revocation by the IRS of the tax-exempt status of the group. In short, the *Harriss* case seems to give a free hand to "grassroots" lobbying; but the IRS seems to say that groups will have to pay for the privilege of exercising that free hand. The question, therefore, remains: what *is* the "intent of Congress"?

The paradox does not end here. Under terms of the 1962 revision of IRS regulations, a business, group, or person, lobbying Congress in its own behalf (or in behalf of a group's members), may deduct lobbying expenses as part of the costs of doing business. But a taxpayer lobbying Congress in behalf of peace, congressional reform, or water purification cannot deduct his expenses—he has no "direct interest" in the issue. Thus, lobbying for self-interest is deductible; lobbying for the public interest is not.[7] Is *this* Congress' true intent? Again, the answer is unclear.

It is not our purpose to discuss ways and means whereby the Lobbying Act might be made more meaningful in relation to the regulation of interest groups' activities. It is sufficient to point out that the Act does not constitute an effective limitation of interest group activity. Provisions of the two Hatch Acts (1925 and 1940), the Taft-Hartley Act (1947), the anti-bribery statute [8] (1962), and Supreme Court rul-

---

[6] King, *op. cit.,* p. 46.

[7] See George D. Webster, *Federal Tax Aspects of Association Activities* (Washington, D.C.: Chamber of Commerce of the United States, 1962) and memorandum from Milton A. Smith, Chamber of Commerce of the United States, "Internal Revenue Service Regulations on Deductibility of Expenses Related to Legislative Activities (April 21, 1965)." For further information on regulation of lobbying expenditures, especially at the state level, see Edgar Lane, *Lobbying and the Law* (Berkeley: University of California Press, 1964).

[8] Public Law 87-849, October 23, 1962. See also the Merchant Marine Act (Section 807) of 1936 and the Foreign Agents Registration Act of 1938 (as amended) for examples of other requirements governing registration of lobbyists.

ings involving the Lobbying Act,[9] similarly fail to provide government with efficient tools for discovering and controlling activities of interest groups.

Proscribed activities are avoided by interest groups, but the forbidden purposes are nevertheless accomplished by other means.

Other governmental pressures have been more effective in limiting pressure from interest groups. Groups are limited by the personal reactions of individual congressmen to the pressures they feel or do not feel. Congressional investigations—or the threat of investigation—can restrain the tempo of lobbying within a certain field. Presidential leadership (and White House lobbying) can counteract interest group pressure.

The ability of Congress to define the problem or to accept a given definition of the problem can—when exercised—exclude all other definitions of the problem and thus determine the limits within which a decision will be reached.

The necessity to preserve cordial relationships with congressional committees and federal agencies limits the freedom of interest groups to lobby their interests unrestrainedly. However, the "capture" of many congressmen and agency personnel by the interest groups they are supposed to regulate lessens the impact of these restraints.

The factor most limiting to effectiveness of interest groups is, perhaps, the sheer weight of thousands of unconnected governmental decisions that *in toto* result in current "policies." These are policies "that are virtually not policies at all but are highly individualized decisions that only by accumulation can be called a policy." [10] Nevertheless, these policies partially define the "rules of the game" and set some questions down as decided, no longer open to debate or pressure. (For example, combinations in restraint of trade are forbidden; the point open to debate is the definition of such a combination.)

Limitation by Non-Governmental Pressures

Fears of the press, of exposure, of the glare of publicity are cited as major reasons why groups might wish to avoid alliances with other groups. The same reasons explain the reluctance of interest groups to engage in activities which, although legal, may be exposed or magnified by the press as being "against the public interest."

Conflict with other groups and the necessity of making the least number of irreconcilable enemies also limit the options open to interest

---

[9] For a brief synopsis, see *CQ, op. cit.,* p. 55.

[10] Theodore Lowi, "American Business, Public Policy, Case-Studies, and Political Theory," *World Politics,* Vol. XVI, No. 4 (July, 1964), pp. 677-715.

groups. Groups compete with other groups in the same field and on the same side (NAM versus Chamber of Commerce of the United States), with groups on opposite sides (NAM versus AFL-CIO), with White House lobbies, with public interest lobbies (Tobacco Institute versus the quasi-governmental lobby of the Interagency Council on Smoking and Health [11]), and, finally, internal factions compete within a single group.

One of Truman's major conclusions is that cohesion in interest groups is inversely proportional to the degree members hold overlapping memberships in other groups. Bauer, Pool, and Dexter's findings challenge this conclusion, stating that cohesion is directly related to overlapping membership; that is, that the existence of multiple groups allows smaller groups to fight openly and hard for a narrow interest, while multi-purpose groups maintain their cohesion by encouraging or permitting these struggles to take place outside the multi-purpose group.[12] These findings are indirectly supported in a letter from the executive vice president of the national Chamber of Commerce:

An affiliated organization, of course, may not be in agreement with a certain National Chamber policy — and may prefer to go its own way and support what it does believe, even though what it believes is contrary to the majority vote of the Chamber's membership.

In such case, the Chamber represents the majority views of its members, and lets those who want to be an exception have their own way. There may be a better strategy than this but, if there is, the Chamber is not at the moment aware of it.[13]

Activities of interest groups are undoubtedly limited by available finances, although there always seems to be enough money available to fight a serious issue. The real financial limitation lies not in the resources available but in the *mobilization* of those resources.[14] Groups have varying abilities to mobilize their resources. This means that the financial power of groups depends upon resources available, success in

---

11 "While nominally a voluntary group of socially conscious citizens, the Council in fact is supported in large measure out of public funds. Hence its advocacy of the findings of the Surgeon General, while sincere, may be viewed as neither disinterested nor free of bias." From "Best Foote [sic] Forward?" *Barron's Magazine*, Vol. XLV, No. 3 (January 18, 1965), p. 1.

12 Raymond A. Bauer, Ithiel de Sola Pool, and Lewis Anthony Dexter, *American Business and Public Policy: The Politics of Foreign Trade* (New York: Atherton Press, 1964), pp. 333-40; © 1963, by permission of Publishers, Atherton Press, all rights reserved.

13 Arch N. Booth, letter to the author, August 11, 1965.

14 Lowi, *op. cit.*, pp. 679-80.

mobilizing those resources, and the ability of the group's leaders to concentrate attention upon an issue sufficiently to call forth the required mobilization.

It has been said many times that lobbying expenditures are "too high." Yet, it appears that the level of expenditures is relative not only to resources and mobilization but to the value that the group puts upon "effective representation."

Thus, the question follows, "What *should* be the cost of effective representation?" The answer depends upon the philosophy adopted. Many critics of interest group activities have expressed dismay that "some men are more able to make their rights meaningful than others. In practical terms, this has meant that those interests with the most to spend for protection have proclaimed 'lobbying for all men' as an almost sacred article of faith. It is not unlike the elephant shouting 'Everybody for himself,' as he stomps up and down among the chickens." [15]

Other critics have said that "the key question is, Do all vital interests get represented? Or does the battle go by default to those with skill and money, and the time to employ them?" [16]

Others have said simply that those who complain about the high costs of lobbying are the poor losers.

The question remains, however, should there be a limit placed on the costs of representation? Should wealthy groups, or groups more successful in mobilizing their resources, be allowed to "price" poorer, less organized groups out of the public opinion and governmental opinion markets? Or, to put it bluntly, is a group entitled to all the "effective representation" it can pay for?

Others argue that the question is not "shall we *limit* interest group activity and expenditures?" but rather "shall we publicize these?" The difficulty with this approach is that publicity itself constitutes an effective limitation on group activity. The U.S. Supreme Court, for example, declared in *NAACP vs. Alabama* (1958) that groups cannot be compelled to divulge membership rosters if such action is likely to cause harassment to the members.

These are questions of value beyond our immediate purposes here. Equality of representation may be impossible in any political situation because of varying intensities of participants (ignoring the problem of non-participants). Yet, democratic theory seems to require that some amount of representation is necessary for all significant groups, through

---

[15] U. S. House of Representatives, Select Committee on Lobbying Activities, *General Interim Report* (House Report 3138), 81st Cong., 2nd Sess. (1950), pp. 23-28.

[16] John P. Roche and Leonard W. Levy, *Parties and Pressure Groups* (New York: Harcourt, Brace & World, 1964), p. 164.

whatever channels control governmental decision-making. If the channel is Congress, then groups should have a vote, member by member. If interest groups are the controlling channel, then all significant groups of citizens should be able to bring pressure to bear through interest groups. But admitting this, the question is no closer to being resolved; additional problems remain: What are "significant" groups? When is an influence channel "controlling"? In short, if one attempts to limit activity and/or expenditures of interest groups, one becomes immediately entangled in the thicket of "representation," a briar patch even the Supreme Court has found impossible to penetrate safely.

There are natural limits to the degree to which interest groups can cooperate with each other. The basis of these limits is the dissimilarity in generic interests of the groups. Yet in the "distributive arena" (Lowi)[17] dissimilarity of interest actually makes coalitions possible, i.e., groups can cooperate on the basis of traded favors. A wilderness-preservation group can cooperate with a travel agents' association to lobby a bill calling for federal support of youth hostels; the travel agents' group will in turn support the wilderness group's bill for establishment of game refuges in the wilderness area.

One of the limits to cooperation among business groups, (according to Bauer, Pool, and Dexter) is the fact that only a minority of businessmen ever feels itself aligned with either side of an issue. If true, Lowi said, "this finding hangs heavy upon the elitists who argue that the top business leaders care and control, and upon the pluralists who assumed that most business leaders are interested and compete."[18] However, one of our findings is that business leaders *do* care, at least enough to meet and discuss in the great secrecy of summit conferences such as the Greenbrier Conference and the Conference of National Organizations. How much coordination and cooperation result from these conferences remains open to question, but the massive drive by business groups favoring the Landrum-Griffin Bill was certainly related to the multiple Greenbrier Conferences held in 1958-1959.

In their study of the Trade Expansion Act, Bauer, Pool, and Dexter conclude that lobbies involved in that controversy were "on the whole poorly financed, ill-managed, out of contact with Congress, and at best only marginally effective in supporting tendencies and measures which already had behind them considerable congressional impetus from other sources."[19]

Perhaps to the academician, the personalities of lobbyists grate on

[17] *Op. cit.,* pp. 688-95.
[18] *Ibid.*
[19] *Op. cit.,* p. 324.

the nerves and are too effusive, or the element of dedication to the public interest is woefully lacking. But "ill-managed" describes fewer than one-quarter of the groups contacted during research for this book. Certainly, criticism can be made of the goals for which many associations work; but the performance of association management often compares favorably with management of any business, social, religious, labor, educational institution or that of other kinds of associations. Certainly, "ill-managed" describes the average university far more accurately than it does, for example, the National Association of Manufacturers.

The real problem is not quality of management but the need for an enlarged concept of "business interest" and "professional interest." The old General Motors definition of "what's good for business" becomes less and less valid as social and industrial integration advance. Business and the professions are becoming less independent of currents in society at large and more dependent upon public support and acceptance—not only of products but also of work practices, wage scales, corporate objectives, professional ethics, fee levels, and so on.

There are many indications that associations are starting to realize this dependency. As Duscha pointed out concerning the program of cooperative lobbying against the Douglas truth in lending bill, to "cover their exposed public relations flank, two high-powered organizations of the small-loan companies shrewdly sought the backing of the American Bar Association, the American Bankers Association, and the U. S. Chamber of Commerce." This was an attempt to "broaden the base of the opposition, for a lobby made up only of those with a crude financial stake in legislation is in a vulnerable position." [20]

Cooperation among interest groups is fostered by recruiting and grooming association leaders who will have frequent dealings with each other. According to Lowi, the process of selection and training of these leaders makes possible "the reduction in a number of basic conflicts among them, and equally makes possible (1) many stable and abiding agreements on policy, (2) accommodation to conflict by more formal, hierarchical means . . . than coalition politics, and (3) settlement of conflict by more informal means . . . that maintain the leaders' legitimacy and stability." [21]

John W. Gardner, Secretary of the Department of Health, Education, and Welfare, reached the conclusion that organizations stagnate because they fail to renew themselves, even though self-renewal in the

---

[20] Julius Duscha, "Your Friendly Finance Company and Its Friends on Capitol Hill," *Harper's Magazine*, Vol. CCXXV, No. 1349 (October, 1962), p. 76.
[21] Lowi, *op. cit.*, p. 680.

organization is continually possible. According to Gardner, there are nine rules to follow if organizational "dry rot" is to be avoided. These rules provide an excellent yardstick by which associations can be compared in terms of internal strength and utilization of management skills, and are summarized (below) as a possible tool for further research in association organization and management.

1. The first rule is that the organization must have an effective program for the recruitment and development of talent.

2. The second rule . . . is that it must be a hospitable environment for the individual.

3. The third rule is that the organization must have built-in provisions for self-criticism.

4. The fourth requirement . . . is fluidity of internal structure.

5. The fifth rule is that the organization must have an adequate system of internal communication.

6. The organization must have some means of combating the process by which men become prisoners of their own procedures.

7. The organization . . . [must] have found some means of combating the vested interests that grow up in every human institution.

8. The eighth rule is that the organization . . . is interested in what it is going to become and not what it has been.

9. An organization runs on motivation, on conviction, on morale. Men have to believe that it really makes a difference whether they do well or badly. They have to care. They have to believe that their efforts as individuals will mean something for the whole organization and will be recognized by the whole organization.[22]

Most business and professional associations are well aware of these "rules," as the next chapter demonstrates. This chapter reports the conclusions of a conference of executives of the national Chamber's Association Committee, held December 4-5, 1964, for the specific purpose of "analyzing, discussing, and predicting the future of associations in the next decade." [23] Representatives of professional, manufacturing, and trade associations participated in the conference convened by the Chamber's Association Service Department.

---

[22] "How to Prevent Organizational Dry Rot," *Harper's Magazine,* Vol. CCXXI, No. 1385 (October, 1965), pp. 20-26.

[23] *Associations in the Next Decade* (Washington, D.C.: Chamber of Commerce of the United States, 1965). (All quotations in the following chapter are taken from this source unless otherwise noted.)

10. The Future of Business and Professional Associations

Governmental Influence on Change in Size and Role

The most compelling force for change—change that will alter the structure, activities, and membership of associations—is that exerted by the federal government.[1] According to association staff and officers, increasing size and complexity of the national government will force business, industry, and the professions to rely more and more upon their associations: "The individual unit simply will not be able to finance the necessary apparatus in Washington or the state capital to represent itself satisfactorily before government agencies or legislative bodies. Those in the private sector of our economy will turn to their respective associations for collective representation."

It has long been postulated (somewhat incorrectly) that Congress prefers to have a bill brought in by a "united front" because such a presentation indicates that conflict has been resolved, and the bill's passage will thus offend no major groups within the industry. Association personnel feel that the same process is a growing characteristic of the executive branch of government, that "government bureaus, already impatient with having to deal with multiple organizations representing various facets of the same industry, will increase the pressure for amalgamation [of associations] . . . More and more, government will *prefer*

---

[1] *Associations in the Next Decade* (Washington, D.C.: Chamber of Commerce of the United States, 1965). (All quotations in this chapter are taken from this source unless otherwise noted.)

to deal with private business through associations." (Emphasis added.)

As mergers within industries reduce the number of significant competing units, so mergers are expected between associations, reducing the numerous overlapping organizations within the same industry and resulting in "umbrella" associations with increased strength, political power, and financial resources. "[Association] members will not accept —financially or intellectually—overlapping programs and services, duplication of efforts, diffused power and other inefficiencies inherent in parallel associations serving the same industry."

Associations are expected to reduce the emphasis they now place on their tax-exempt status. Many association executives already feel that "the tax exempt status is not essential to the ultimate accomplishment of association objectives, and in some cases might even be detrimental." Many associations will begin to operate "totally or in part as profit making corporations . . . paying income taxes on all or portions of their income."

One of the methods by which government will compel change is through competition between government services and association activities. "Today, we are seeing a growing number of instances where government has entered the association field by providing services for business, industry and the professions which have customarily been the responsibility of voluntary associations." Functions and services of the Employment Security Division of the Department of Labor, for example, have led the department into direct competition with private employment agencies. Government research often duplicates research programs of associations, frequently at a wage scale making the association's research positions financially unattractive. "Continued expansion of government services and programs, especially those developed in conjunction with industry or professional groups, will result in direct competition with associations unless association leaders continue to oppose the government's encroachment into areas better handled by private means. There is nothing to stop the government from by-passing the association and absorbing its activities once the association's brains have been picked by the government agency or department. . . ."

Associations are well aware of the uses and abuses of advisory committees in which government participates: "There is little doubt that there will be an increase in the importance and frequency of association and industry liaison with the Federal Government, especially with the regulatory agencies and various departments . . . This area encompasses the relationship between associations and the Federal Government with respect to government-industry advisory committees and educational liaison between associations and government."

To retain control of issues and personnel involved in advisory committees, associations recommend two "guidelines":

1. Insist that meetings with government groups be conducted in accordance with mutually agreeable ground rules. Both parties should agree upon a formal agenda with a list of representatives to attend from both sides. . . .

2. Before any meeting is held . . . there should be a meeting of the minds on publicity before and after the meeting . . . .

Association executives apparently do not expect either a more favorable or a more hostile attitude to be displayed by the Internal Revenue Service: "Undoubtedly nonprofit associations in the immediate future will witness increasing pressure from the Internal Revenue Service . . . [on the other hand] associations do not expect any radical changes in the regulations affecting the tax exempt status of associations or the deductibility of dues paid to associations." This expectation could be radically altered at any time by legislation concerning tax-exempt organizations.

Other Forces Stimulating Change in Size or Role

As the size of other groups—unions, schools, churches, government, etc.—increases, the size of trade and professional associations will also increase; and new techniques for management of resulting "umbrella" associations will have to be developed. Association executives expect to see greater use made of "multiple association management" techniques by which the physical administration of association routine work is contracted to management firms which will concurrently manage several associations.

It should be emphasized that "management" applies here to administration only, not to policy formation. As a step toward this technique, associations are already demonstrating increased willingness to employ outside experts and consultants. Although not discussed during the national Chamber's conference, it is doubtful that lobbying will be contracted to a professional lobbying association, since lobbying is normally thought of by associations as part of the policy, not the administrative, process. However, success of professional lobbying firms (such as Whitaker and Baxter) may encourage the development and use of professional firms. It is more probable that as associations merge and grow in size, larger staffs will be hired—with a commensurately larger quota of lobbyists.

According to association executives, the individual member will not "lose his individual identification and become alienated from the organization. Quite the contrary! The super association will demand greater participation by more people than ever before. A greater personal involvement is likely since the association will assume much greater importance in their business scope. Members will become more involved, for the association's success will mean business life or death for them."

Elements Needed by the New "Super Associations"

Increased membership participation has already been cited as the first essential element with new associations. The second element is improvement in the quality of association staff.

In education and training, most association executives came to the field through some other job or responsibility. This required self-training, learning by experience, and self-improvement of association management skills.

There will be greater demand for those with liberal arts education and more opportunity for generalists than specialists. While degrees and titles may impress members, and provide "pegs" for hiring and compensating, association executives will find specially tailored short courses, meetings, and so forth to be of increasing value to them....

There will not be as many top jobs for association executives in the future, but there will be more opportunities for second and third men, and department heads. The department head tomorrow will be far better off prestige-wise, and responsibility-wise than the executive of a small association today.

The new super associations of tomorrow will encounter greater problems in policy formation, according to today's association executives.

It will be difficult to guarantee that an association's policies are properly based. Assurance that all segments of the big association are represented in policy matters will be essential. A corollary problem will be one of internal politics. With the giant association will come ambition for elected office. The association will have to make certain that policy is controlled by seasoned people, for the organization's influence will be vast.

Committees will tend to become bodies of technicians and specialists, assisted by highly qualified staff people. Tomorrow's association will be faced with serious personnel problems in attempting to attract and retain qualified executives.

Finally, preparation and presentation of material to legislative bodies and regulatory agencies will demand closer contacts with agency officials and congressmen. In the continuing struggle between big associations and big government, the associations recognize that theirs is the smaller power and that they therefore must be always able to play a strongly defensive role. "Direct contact with elected legislators and influential members of legislative committees having authority over or influence upon such agencies may prove to be the best recourse in an adverse situation." The "one-man" association will continue to exist, but "its role will be largely as a defensive lobbyist."

The report of this conference convened by the national Chamber of Commerce can be summarized in the words of one of the panel discussion leaders:

> So this is how we see the association of America in 1975 pertaining particularly to their structure, activities and membership. The concentration already begun will bring about the super association, establishing policies and representing itself before government, organized labor and the public on behalf of an entire industry. In the next decade, we will have the corporate association. It will be vastly more effective in its total than its various uncoordinated components are today. It will be efficiently managed and well financed. The association of 1975 will directly reflect the sophistication of the industry or profession it serves.

That these words echo the corporate statism of Mussolini does not seem to have occurred to the association executives, or, if it did, the ready apology presumably would have been, "We are being forced into it by big government." At no point in the printed report of conference discussions is there any hesitancy shown by association executives regarding the roles they feel they will be called upon to play by 1975. No embarrassment is evident in their acceptance of "collective representation." No reluctance is indicated in their agreement that competitive pressure will be another influence for association consolidation; this is described instead as "hard-hitting business sense." An association executive, it is predicted, will "guide his organization as closely as possible in conformity with his industry's pattern." It will become increasingly important "for associations to coordinate their efforts with other associations having common objectives so the agencies cannot apply the 'divide and conquer' tactic."

It appears from this examination of the future of associations,[2] as

---

[2] Business associations are not alone in considering amalgamation: "Mergers are now under consideration by more than a score of unions operating in major industries . . . Merger-minded union chiefs figure combining forces will strengthen their bargaining power, end jurisdictional rivalries and permit more ambitious organizing drives . . .

"'The "conglomerate union" . . . may be the labor organization of the future.' suggests Jack Conway, executive director of the AFL-CIO's Industrial Union

predicted by association executives themselves, that a great deal of the furor over "competition," "free enterprise," and "centralized government" is propaganda generated by associations to attract the attention and favorable emotional reaction of their members.

If, as association personnel claim, associations reflect the desires of their members, then American businessmen and professional men are not as alarmed about giant government as is commonly supposed. At least, the associations representing these men are not alarmed about bigness or centralization. On the contrary, they are making plans to centralize and participate and—if possible—play commanding roles in a society in which giants face each other in constant competition, while the individual is to have only the choice of participating in the super associations or suffering economic and political isolation. Members not only *will* become more involved in associations, they *must* become involved, for as the conference report indicates, "the association's success will mean business life or death for them."

This is a strange vision of the "competitive, free enterprise, market economy" world to be held by—for example—members of the Chamber of Commerce of the United States. It may be that business and professional associations have at last agreed that (as one conference participant stated): "[We must] lead [our] organization in dealing with 'things as they are,' and not live by the old clichés. We must chase the unicorns from our gardens."

Areas for Future Research

Two areas of lobbying activities obviously require a great deal more attention than they have received. The first is the creation and operation of White House lobbies, that is, lobbying of national, state, and local governments by representatives of the executive branch of the federal government.

According to Richard Harwood, White House lobbies "are used for the same reason that private companies pay large sums to sports and entertainment figures—to give testimonials and to lend their prestige to a product. The difference is that in the case of White House front

---

Department. [IUD] . . . The IUD also is giving thought to sponsoring a sort of super-union, not requiring actual merger of individual unions but tying together several in a well-financed organization that would negotiate with major corporations and industries . . .

"A more sweeping restructuring of organized labor is proposed by Ralph Helstein [President of United Packing House Workers of America]. 'My idea is that there shouldn't be any more than ten or fifteen unions in the U.S. . . . There should be one transportation union, a metal-trades union, a food-and-drink union, and so on.'" James P. Gannon, "Labor Organizations Show Mounting Interest in Combining Forces," *Wall Street Journal* (March 7, 1968), pp. 1-2.

groups, the product is political and the public is unaware of the relationship." [3] Harwood cited the example of government support of the National Council of Senior Citizens: "An example of this practice [support of Administration objectives with public funds] under President Kennedy was the assignment of Federal officials to prepare materials, including radio tapes, for use in the campaign for Medicare by the National Council of Senior Citizens. During this period, the National Council was directly subsidized—at Kennedy's direction—by the Democratic National Committee." [4]

A second example, to the author even more disturbing, is the creation and support, by public funds, of the National Interagency Council on Smoking and Health. The National Council calls itself "a voluntary association of national agencies and organizations to combat smoking as a health hazard," [5] but there is nothing voluntary about the use of tax funds to support Council operations. For example, the United States Public Health Service's Division of Chronic Diseases "awarded $14,456 to the University of Oklahoma Bureau of Public Health Research, Oklahoma City, for the project's first year of operations . . . [to] develop and demonstrate effective *methods of influencing attitudes* of elementary and high school students toward smoking and health. Grant funds will make it possible to maintain a *permanent office and staff* to assemble and coordinate activities of member groups of the State Interagency Council on Smoking and Health." [6]

This "voluntary" association has thus tapped federal funds to create a permanent office and staff with the avowed purpose of propagandizing taxpayers and their children to change their attitudes and tastes. As Senator Morton would say, "If cigarettes today, will it be tailfins, books, and movies tomorrow?" At best, this appears to be highly questionable use of taxpayers' funds.

A second lobbying activity in need of further research is the role of lobbies as "middlemen" between the executive branch and Congress ("clientele lobbying"). The following statement, by an American Bankers Association staff member, illustrates this function:

The American Bankers Association frequently finds itself in the

---

[3] From the personal notes of Richard Harwood, Washington correspondent for the *Louisville Courier-Journal.*

[4] Harwood, "Special Interests *vs.* the Public Good?" *Louisville Courier-Journal,* October 10, 1965.

[5] "Smoking and Health Newsletter" (Bethesda, Maryland: National Interagency Council on Smoking and Health), Vol. I, No. 1 (July-August, 1965), p. 8.

[6] "$14,000 Campaign Aimed at Cigaret Education," *Oklahoma City Advertiser,* July 29, 1965. Emphasis supplied.

middle between Treasury and Congress. The Treasury will come to us and say, "Look, fellows, we need this legislation. Can you help us work with Congress to make sure that it is passed?" Or a delegation from Congress will come to us and say, "Look, fellows, can you get the Treasury to issue a certain regulation?" We were exactly in this middleman position during the controversy over the change-over from silver coins.[7]

Another example of the middleman role of the lobby was the campaign to establish uniform daylight saving time. The Transportation Association of America was the lobby-in-the-middle although, this time, opposing sides were both in Congress. Some farm and outdoor amusement associations opposed the bill; other outdoor amusement groups and the transportation associations supported the bill and lobbied it to successful passage.

It is the author's hope that this presentation has avoided giving an impression that lobbying is always formally and intellectually structured by logical organization and rational decision. Many decisions leading to lobbying actions appear to be made below the level of deliberate consciousness and may depend as much upon personalities and habits as upon any rational estimation of group strategy, needs and resources. To this extent, it is difficult to discover the pattern, regularity, or reason in interest group behavior.

Intergroup lobbying and direct lobbying of Congress are professional activities for lobbyists of the business and professional associations interviewed by the author; but these professional techniques are not learned in colleges or at institutes; they are learned on the job, by trial and error. The participants act and react according to their own experience; thus, the quality and type of experience acquired before they undertake lobbying help determine their actions as lobbyists.

A great deal of thought and planning goes into lobbying activities, but, nevertheless, many crucial decisions are probably based on no more than one man's guess as to how another will vote, or one man's ability to estimate and appraise the character and potential of another.

Lobbying, like all politics, is a game of individual players in which the "feel for the game" is all-important, and in which group action is often the product of skillful manipulation by a few astute directors.

Therefore, one meaningful criterion for measuring one interest group against another might be, "How well does each group allow its lobbyists to make the best use of its (the group's) resources?" Or, nega-

---

[7] Interview with Paul Collins, Washington, D.C., June 17, 1965.

tively, "To what extent are logically desirable group lobbying activities restricted or prohibited by group policies, membership, and/or staff?" In this work only preliminary answers to these questions have been put forth. Much more research is needed—a great deal of it utilizing survey research techniques—before these questions can be answered in full.

If future studies of lobbying activities are to avoid the "horror" approach, scholars will have to accept lobbies as inevitable, desirable, or both.

It is the author's conclusion that lobbies are both inevitable and desirable. As Charles Frankel said, "That aspect of democracy which most regularly troubles its partisans—the open struggle among special interests—is precisely what marks democracy as a system resting on the consent of the governed. The politics of pressure groups is the essential feature of the politics of democracy. The only alternative to the politics of pressure groups is government that rules over isolated and rootless individuals who have no groups other than government to protect them and no autonomous social power of their own." [8]

The problem, of course, is to ensure that "consent of the governed" does not become only the consent of those who are best able to *express* that consent, or those who can prevent action by withholding consent. To the degree that interest groups mobilize, grant, and withhold consent, they are both vehicles *of* and roadblocks *to* legislation and other forms of political decisions. If greater expression of consent or dissent (i.e., participation) is necessary to make democracy more efficient, then interest groups must be encouraged to organize and to operate openly. If the difficulty lies in the inordinate power of some groups at a certain time, then one solution could be mobilization of other groups to compete for that power.

Democracy cannot be made to work by *restricting* individual or group expressions of consent or dissent. On this truth, history is clear.

---

[8] *The Democratic Prospect* (Colophon edition, New York: Harper & Row, 1964), pp. 46-47.

Part 5
Appendix

Appendix

GUIDE FOR INDIVIDUAL RESEARCH

1. What systems exist for classifying groups according to structure, form, and purpose? How does Group X differ from others in form and/or type? What similarities exist among all forms of organized groups? Which of these differences and similarities are significant in that they materially aid in distinguishing Group X from other groups? How does internal form or organization affect the internal procedures and processes within the group? How can (or has) an "active minority" gain(ed) control of a group? What significance does this have? What advantages and disadvantages are concurrent with the organizational form of Group X (i.e., federated, unitary, ad hoc, committee form, etc.)?

2. In what ways has Group X, over time, changed its structure, strategies, degree of access, or degree of cohesion — as a result of changes in American democratic institutions, social and/or legal environment, and changes in public opinion? Have these institutions, environments, and public attitudes, in turn, been changed themselves as a result of the operations of pressure groups, particularly Group X? How well is Group X adapting to environmental changes? Is the group more — or less — accepted in recent years as "good" within the framework of our culture? Why?

3. What does Group X consider as its primary goals, in broad-scale terms? Have its goals changed since (for example) the New Deal? The advent of federal regulatory agencies? Does Group X now seek something more or different than mere "access"? Does the group have a clear picture of its own objectives?

4. What are Group X's relationships with the political parties? Is Group X just one of an aggregate of special interest groups forming a majority under the name "party"? Is the group superior or inferior to the party toward which it feels the closest loyalty? Does Group X have reasonable access to *both* parties at federal *and* state levels?

5. To what extent are Group X's goals, image, strategies, structure, and successes or failures determined by the group's personnel policy — that is, the method used to recruit, train, and assign employees and lobbyists? What are the requirements Group X seeks in its lobbyists?

6. What relationship do leadership skills have to the kinds of leaders selected by Group X? To the kinds of procedures used to select these leaders? Is there "democracy" in the relations among group leaders? Between leaders and membership?

7. To what extent is Group X's environment peopled with actual or potential allies and with potential groups which are not yet organized? What effect do these groups have on the ability of Group X to modify or control its own environment? To push for certain policies or actions?

8. What motives exist for cooperation between Group X and potential allies? What obstacles or negative motives may there be to cooperation between them? What groups find it difficult or impossible to form alliances with Group X — and why?

9. To what extent is a given political situation dominated by cooperation among major groups, not by competition among them? If this cooperation exists, is there sufficient public force to make them accountable? What kind of public forces?

10. In what arena(s) will Group X be most likely to make its play — or will it be likely to use more than one arena? Why? What factors govern whether Group X will lobby the bureaucracy, Congress, state legislatures, the courts, the executive, or the public directly? In what ways and for what reasons does Group X's lobbying at the state level differ from its lobbying at the national level?

11. To what extent will Group X find opposition to its desires from the bureaucracy at any level? What kinds of goals may the bureaucracy have that conflict with those of the group? On the other hand, why might bureaucracy cooperate with this pressure group? What sort of limits operate to restrict the bureaucracy in the degree it can support or oppose the group's goals? What limits similarly operate to restrict the freedom of the executive,

judiciary, and legislature in the degree they can support or oppose Group X's goals?

12. What relationship exists between the ideology of Group X and its goals, structure, chances for success? Is the ideology "valid" in the sense of being current, logical, correspondent to reality?

13. Does (or will) a study of Group X tell us anything valuable about the formation of public policy? Does such a study help (a) explain the working of the political party system, (b) aid students or publics in preventing monopolization of the decision-making process, (c) lessen the chances of minority rule by an economic or power "elite"?

Bibliography

BOOKS AND PAMPHLETS

Agar, Herbert. *The Price of Union.* Boston, Houghton Mifflin Company, 1950. 750 pp.

Bauer, Raymond A., Ithiel de Sola Pool, and Lewis Anthony Dexter, *American Business and Public Policy: The Politics of Foreign Trade.* New York, Atherton Press, 1964. 499 pp.

Cater, Douglas. *The Fourth Branch of Government.* Vintage edition. New York, Alfred A. Knopf and Random House, 1965. 194 pp.

Congressional Quarterly Service. *Congressional Quarterly Almanac 1962.* Washington, D.C., Congressional Quarterly Service, 1963. 1102 pp.

————. *Legislators and the Lobbyists.* Washington, D.C., Congressional Quarterly Service, 1965. 78 pp.

Deakin, James. *The Lobbyists.* Washington, D.C., Public Affairs Press, 1966. 309 pp.

Duncan, Delbert J. (ed.). *Trade Association Management.* Chicago, National Institute for Commercial and Trade Organization Executives, 1948. 190 pp.

Frankel, Charles. *The Democratic Prospect.* Colophon edition. New York, Harper & Row, 1964. 222 pp.

Harris, Richard. *The Real Voice.* New York, Macmillan Company, 1964. 245 pp.

Katz, Elihu, and Paul F. Lazarsfeld. *Personal Influence.* Glencoe, Free Press, 1955. 400 pp.

Kelley, Stanley. *Professional Public Relations and Political Power.* Baltimore, Johns Hopkins Press, 1956. 247 pp.

Key, V. O., Jr. *Politics, Parties, and Pressure Groups.* Fourth edition. New York, Thomas Y. Crowell Company, 1962. 783 pp.

Lane, Edgar. *Lobbying and the Law.* Berkeley, University of California Press, 1964. 224 pp.

Lipset, Seymour Martin. *Political Man: The Social Bases of Politics.* Anchor edition. Garden City, Doubleday & Company, 1963. 477 pp. (Originally published 1960.)

McConnell, Grant. *Private Power and American Democracy.* New York, Alfred A. Knopf, 1966. 397 pp.

McCune, Wesley. *Who's Behind Our Farm Policy?* New York, Frederick A. Praeger, Inc., 1956. 374 pp.

McKean, Dayton D. *Party and Pressure Politics.* Boston, Houghton Mifflin Company, 1949. 712 pp.

Matthews, Donald R. *U. S. Senators and Their World.* Caravelle edition. New York, Random House, 1960. 303 pp.

Milbrath, Lester W. *The Washington Lobbyists.* Chicago, Rand, McNally & Co., 1963. 431 pp.

Monsen, R. Joseph, and Mark W. Cannon. *The Makers of Public Policy: American Power Groups and Their Ideologies.* New York, McGraw-Hill Book Company, 1965. 355 pp.

Odegard, Peter. *Pressure Politics.* New York, Columbia University Press, 1928. 299 pp.

Riggs, Fred W. *Pressures on Congress: A Study of the Repeal of Chinese Exclusion.* New York, King's Crown Press, 1950. 260 pp.

Roche, John P. and Leonard W. Levy. *Parties and Pressure Groups.* New York, Harcourt, Brace & World, Inc., 1964. 239 pp.

Schattschneider, E. E. *The Semisovereign People.* New York, Holt, Rinehart and Winston, 1960. 147 pp.

Stern, Philip M. *The Great Treasury Raid.* New York, Random House, 1964. 361 pp.

Thoré, Eugene M. *Lobbying as a Function of Business and Government.* Bloomington, Indiana University Graduate School of Business (Bureau of Business Research), 1964. 17 pp.

de Tocqueville, Alexis. *Democracy in America.* Phillips Bradley edition. New York, Alfred A. Knopf, 1945. Vol. I. 231 pp.

Truman, David B. *The Governmental Process: Political Interests and Public Opinion.* Sixth edition. New York, Alfred A. Knopf, 1965. 544 pp. (Originally published 1951.)

World Almanac 1966. New York, New York World-Telegram Corp., 1966. 896 pp.

Zeigler, Harmon. *Interest Groups in American Society.* Third printing. Englewood Cliffs, Prentice-Hall, Inc., 1965. 343 pp.

PERIODICALS AND NEWSPAPERS

Anderson, Totton J. "Pressure Groups and Intergovernmental Relations." *The Annals* (American Academy of Political and Social Science), Vol. CCCLIX (May, 1965), pp. 116-126.

Barron, John. "The Case of Bobby Baker and the Courageous Senator." *Reader's Digest,* Vol. LXXXVII, No. 521 (September, 1965), pp. 112-118.

Bagdikian, Ben H. and Don Oberdorfer. "Bobby Was the Boy to See." *Saturday Evening Post,* Vol. CCXXXVI, No. 43 (December 7, 1963), pp. 26-29.

Congressional Quarterly Service. "AMA Breaking All Records for Lobby Spending." *Washington Post,* June 23, 1965.

_____. "Lobby Campaign Pushed for Dirksen Amendment." *Congressional Quarterly Weekly Report.* Vol. XXIII, No. 32 (Week ending August 6, 1965), pp. 1569-1575.

Deakin, James. "NAM to Set Up a Pro-Business Campaign Unit." *St. Louis Post-Dispatch,* April 24, 1963.

Drew, Elizabeth Brenner. "The Quiet Victory of the Cigarette Lobby." *Atlantic Monthly,* Vol. CCXVI, No. 3 (September, 1965), pp. 76-80.

Duscha, Julius. "Your Friendly Finance Company and Its Friends on Capitol Hill." *Harper's Magazine,* Vol. CCXXV, No. 1349 (October, 1962), pp. 75-78.

Evans, Rowland and Robert Novak. "Crisis Over 14(b)." *Washington Post,* August 25, 1965.

Freyman, John Gordon. "A Doctor Prescribes for the AMA." *Harper's Magazine,* Vol. CCXXXI, No. 1383 (August, 1965), pp. 76-80.

Gardner, John W. "How to Prevent Organizational Dry Rot." *Harper's Magazine,* Vol. CCXXXI, No. 1385 (October, 1965), pp. 20-26.

Harwood, Richard. "Special Interests *vs.* the Public Good?" *Louisville Courier-Journal,* October 10, 1965.

_____. "Lobbyists Tied to U. S. Sugar Policy." *Louisville Courier-Journal,* October 11, 1965.

_____. "Special Interest Groups Have A Way of Collecting." *Louisville Courier-Journal,* October 12, 1965.

_____. "President Doesn't Switch Nor Fight Tobacco Congressmen." *Louisville Courier-Journal,* October 13, 1965.

_____. "The Washington Lawyers." Written for the *Louisville Courier-Journal* in 1965 but not published.

King, Larry. "Washington's Money Birds." *Harper's Magazine,* Vol. CCXXXI, No. 1383 (August, 1965), pp. 45-54.

Knoll, Erwin. "Our 'Model T' Copyright Law." *Reporter,* Vol. XXXVI, No. 5 (March 10, 1966), pp. 39-41.

Kotz, Nick. " 'The Coalition' Works to Reelect New Iowa Democrats in Congress." *Des Moines Register,* July 6, 1965. (Reprinted in *Congressional Record,* July 7, 1965, p. 15247.)

Latham, Earl. "The Group Basis of Politics: Notes for a Theory." *American Political Science Review,* Vol. XLVI, No. 2 (June, 1952), pp. 76-97.

Lowi, Theodore. "American Business, Public Policy, Case-Studies and Political Theory." *World Politics,* Vol. XVI, No. 4 (July, 1964), pp. 677-715.

Milbrath, Lester W. "Lobbying as a Communications Process." *Public Opinion Quarterly,* Vol. XXIV (Spring, 1960), pp. 32-53.

Nossiter, Bernard D. "Labor Bill Lobby: Mood Manipulation is Given Credit." *Washington Post,* September 10, 1959.

Novak, Robert. "Two Business Groups Split Over Interest Rate Disclosure Bill." *Wall Street Journal,* April 13, 1960.

Novak, Robert. "Changes Mulled in Bill to Show Finance Charges." *Wall Street Journal,* April 18, 1960.

Oberdorfer, Don. "The New Political Non-Job." *Harper's Magazine,* Vol. CCXXXI, No. 1385 (October, 1965), pp. 108-19.

Pearson, Drew. "Senate Bows to Drug Companies." *Washington Post,* July 12, 1965.

————. "Dirksen, Douglas Near Showdown." *Washington Post,* August 4, 1965.

————. "Liberty Lobby Guns for Fortas." *Washington Post,* August 5, 1965.

Pincus, Walter. "Foreign Lobbyists Fight Hard for 4 Million-Ton Sugar Pie." *Washington* (D.C.) *Star,* August 23, 1965.

Poole, Daniel. "Real Estate Bill Called Detrimental to Industry." *Washington* (D.C.) *Star,* June 25, 1965.

Smith, David G. "Pragmatism and the Group Theory of Politics." *American Political Science Review,* LVIII, No. 3 (September, 1964), pp. 600-610.

Smith, Desmond. "American Radio Today." *Harper's Magazine,* Vol. CCXXIX, No. 1372 (September, 1964), pp. 59-63.

Steele, Jack. "Senate Opponents Promise Bitter Fight on Sugar Bill." *Rocky Mountain News,* October 14, 1965.

Stern, Laurence. "Douglas *vs.* Dirksen In the Big Debate." *Washington Post,* August 4, 1965.

Turner, Harry A. "How Pressure Groups Operate." *The Annals* (American Academy of Political and Social Science), Vol. CCCXIX (September, 1958), pp. 63-72.

Wilson, Richard. "Congress Goes on a Law-Making Binge." *Washington* (D.C.) *Star,* August 18, 1965.

Zeller, Belle. "Regulation of Pressure Groups and Lobbyists." *The Annals* (American Academy of Political and Social Science), Vol. CCCXIX (September, 1958), pp. 94-103.

Barron's Magazine, Vol. XLV, No. 3 (January 18, 1965), p. 1. "Best Foote Forward?"

Commonweal, Vol. XXXI, No. 52 (March 11, 1965), p. 3. "Packaged Truth."

Denver Post, February 10, 1966. "Jobless Pay Labor Goal."

————, April 1, 1966. "Who Bankrolls Dirksen Amendment Drive?"

Fortune, Vol. XXXVIII, No. 1 (July, 1948), pp. 72-75, 165-69, "Renovation in NAM."

Newsweek, Vol. LXVII, No. 6 (February 7, 1966), p. 57. "Business Trends."

Time, Vol. LXXXVII, No. 9 (March 4, 1966), p. 27. "A Family Quarrel."

Yale Law Journal, Vol. LXIII, No. 7 (May, 1954), pp. 938-1022. "The American Medical Association: Power, Purpose, and Politics in Organized Medicine."

ORGANIZATIONS: OCCASIONAL PUBLICATIONS
(Place of Publication is Washington, D.C.,
unless otherwise noted.)

American Bankers Association. *Banking Legislation in the Second Session, 88th Congress.* 1965. 36 pp.

American Bar Association. *Presidential Inability and Vice Presidential Vacancy.* 1964. 30 pp.

American Farm Bureau Federation. *Farm Bureau Policies for 1965.* 1964. 59 pp.

Chamber of Commerce of the United States. *A Glimpse of the National Chamber 1964–1965.* 1964. 59 pp.

———. *Associations in the Next Decade.* 1965. 12 pp.

———. *Basic Operating Policies of Trade and Professional Associations.* 1960. 46 pp.

———. *Congressional Handbook 1965: 89th Congress, First Session.* 1965. 43 pp.

———. *Congressional Issue Study: The Packaging-Labeling Controls Bill (S. 985).* 1965. 46 pp.

———. *Federal Regulation of Business: Where Do We Go From Here?* 1964. 25 pp.

———. *Federal Tax Aspects of Association Activities (With 1962 Supplements).* 1962. 114 pp.

———. *Finding and Applying Private-Business Solutions to National Problems.* 1965. 32 pp.

———. *Legislative Handbook for Associations.* 1962. 40 pp.

———. *Let's Talk About Labor.* 1963. 28 pp.

———. *National Legislative Issue Interests of Member Trade and Professional Associations of the Chamber of Commerce of the United States.* 1964. 88 pp.

———. *National Chamber and How It Works in the Public Interest, The.* 1960. 60 pp.

———. *Officers, Directors, and Committeemen 1964–1965.* 1964. 75 pp.

———. *Organization Members of Chamber of Commerce of the United States.* 1965. 97 pp.

———. *Our First Fifty Years.* 1962. 26 pp.

———. *Policy Declarations 1964–1965.* 1964. 149 pp.

———. *Policy Declarations 1965–1966.* 1965. 150 pp.

———. *Trade and Professional Association Members of the National Chamber.* 1963. 171 pp.

Conference of National Organizations. *A Brief History.* 1962. 9 pp.

Food Group, The. *Membership Directory.* 1965. 22 pp.

National Association of Broadcasters. *1964 Major Issues and Projects: Special Report to the NAB Membership.* 1964. 47 pp.

National Automobile Dealers Association. *The Franchised New Car and Truck Dealer Story.* 1965. 53 pp.

National Canners Association. *Annual Report of the Executive Vice President.* 1964. 64 pp.

————. *Why Should A Canner Belong to the N.C.A. Circa* 1965. 7 pp.

National Small Business Association. *The Truth About "Truth-in-Lending."* 1965. 72 pp.

ORGANIZATIONS: PERIODICAL PUBLICATIONS
(Place of Publication is Washington, D.C.,
unless otherwise noted.)

American Bankers Association. *Banking.* Weekly.

————. *Washington Bulletin.* Monthly.

American Bar Association. *Washington Letter.* Monthly.

American Farm Bureau Federation. *Farm Bureau News.* Weekly.

Chamber of Commerce of the United States. *Association Letter.* Monthly.

————. *Chamber of Commerce Newsletter.* Monthly.

————. *Congressional Action.* Weekly when Congress is in session.

————. *Here's the Issue.* Biweekly when Congress is in session.

————. *Nation's Business.* Monthly.

————. *Special Report.* Published irregularly on topics of legislative importance.

————. *Washington Report.* Weekly.

Information Committee on Federal Food Regulations. Untitled newsletter or memorandum. Washington, D.C., Information Committee on Federal Food Regulations, 1963–1965, selected dates.

National Association of Manufacturers. *NAM Reports.* Weekly.

National Association of Manufacturers. *NAM Reports in Depth.* Weekly.

National Small Business Association. *Small Business Bulletin.* Monthly.

ORGANIZATIONS: ARTICLES IN PERIODICALS
(Place of publication is Washington, D.C.,
unless otherwise noted.)

Adams, Charles F. "Effective Action by Businessmen." *NAM Reports in Depth,* Vol. X, No. 16 (April 19, 1965), pp. 13-14.

Backstrand, Clifford J. "What BIPAC Can Do For American Business." *NAM Reports in Depth,* Vol. X, No. 20 (May 27, 1965), p. 11.

Consumer Reports, Vol. XXX, No. 3 (March, 1965), pp. 1-4. "A Story for Our Times." (Consumers Union)

Nation's Business, Vol. LIII, No. 3 (March, 1965), pp. 34-37. "Who Says Shoppers Are Stupid?" (Chamber of Commerce of the United States)

GOVERNMENT DOCUMENTS

U.S. Senate. Subcommittee on Production and Stabilization, Committee on Banking and Currency. *Hearings on Truth in Lending: S. 1740.* 87th Cong., 2nd Sess. (May 8, 10-11, 15-18, 1962).

_____. Subcommittee on Production and Stabilization, Committee on Banking and Currency. *Hearings on Truth in Lending: S. 750.* Two vols. 88th Cong., 1st Sess. (August 16-17, 23-24, November 22, 1963; January 11, 1964).

_____. Subcommittee on Antitrust and Monopoly, Committee on the Judiciary. *Hearings on Packaging and Labeling Practices: S. Res. 52.* 87th Cong., 1st Sess. (June 28-30, October 25-27, December 14-15, 1961).

_____. Subcommittee on Antitrust and Monopoly, Committee on the Judiciary. *Report* [pursuant to S. Res. 262] *on Truth in Packaging.* 88th Cong., 2nd Sess. (August 4, 1964).

_____. Subcommittee on Constitutional Amendments, Committee on the Judiciary. *Hearings on Reapportionment of State Legislatures: S. J. Res. 2, etc.* 89th Cong., 1st Sess. (March 3-5, 9-11, 17-18, April 27-29, May 5-7, 14, 20-21, 1965).

_____. Special Committee to Investigate Political Activities, Lobbying, and Campaign Contributions. *Final Report* [Report No. 395]. 85th Cong., 1st Sess. (May 31, 1957).

_____. Committee on Foreign Relations. *Hearings on Activities of Non-diplomatic Representatives of Foreign Principals in the United States.* 88th Cong., 1st Sess. (February 4, 6, 1963).

_____. Subcommittee on Constitutional Amendments, Committee on the Judiciary. *Hearings on Presidential Inability and Vacanies in the Office of Vice President: S. J. Res. 1.* 89th Cong., 1st Sess. (January 29, 1965).

_____. Committee on Interior and Insular Affairs and Committee on Public Works. *Joint Hearings on Water Resources Planning Act of 1961.* 87th Cong., 1st Sess. (July 26 and August 16, 1961).

_____. Committee on Commerce. *Hearings on Cigarette Labeling and Advertising: S. 559 and S. 547.* 89th Cong., 1st Sess. (March 22-25, 29-30, April 1-2, 1965).

U.S. House of Representatives. Committee on Interstate and Foreign Commerce. *Hearings on Cigarette Labeling and Advertising—1965: H.R. 2248, etc.* 89th Cong., 1st Sess. (April 6-9, 13-15, May 4, 1965).

_____. War on Poverty Subcommittee of Education and Labor Committee. *Hearings on H.R. 10440, Economic Opportunity Act of 1964.* 88th Cong., 2nd Sess. (March 17-20, April 7-10, 13-14).

_____. Special Subcommittee on Labor, Committee on Education and Labor. *Hearings on Section 14(b) of the Labor-Management Relations Act: H.R. 77, etc.* 89th Cong., 1st Sess. (May 24-28, June 1-4, 8, 1965).

_____. Select Committee on Lobbying Activities. *General Interim Report* [House Report 3138]. 81st Cong., 2nd Sess. (October 20, 1950).

_____. Committee on Banking and Currency. *Hearings on Meetings with Department and Agency Officials, and Trade Organizations.* 88th Cong., 1st Sess. (January 29-31, February 5-7, 18-20, 1963).

U.S. Senate. Committee on Government Operations. *Availability of Information from Federal Departments and Agencies* [House Report 918]. 88th Cong., 1st Sess. (November 22, 1963).

Congressional Record. Daily edition. Washington, D.C., Gov't. Printing Office.

Federal Register. Vol. 30, No. 75 (April 20, 1965).

INTERVIEWS: ORGANIZATION PERSONNEL

(All interviews took place in Washington, D.C.,
between June 5 and September 14, 1965.)

Beck, Lowell. Assistant Director, Washington Office, American Bar Association.

Channell, Donald. Director, Washington Office, American Bar Association.

Collins, Paul. Executive Staff, American Bankers Association.

Comstock, Paul. General Counsel, National Association of Broadcasters.

Cope, James. Executive Staff, Proprietary Association.

Elliott, Warren. Assistant Counsel, Life Insurance Association of America.

Heffelfinger, William T. Federal Administrative Adviser, American Bankers Association.

Heiney, Robert. Director, Government-Industry Relations Division, National Canners Association.

Liebenson, Herbert. Executive Staff, National Small Business Association.

Nellor, Ed. National Right to Work Committee.

Newman, Mrs. Sarah H. General Secretary, National Consumers League.

Roberts, Clyde. Executive Staff, National Association of Manufacturers.

Rolphe, John F. III. Assistant to the Federal Legislative Counsel, American Bankers Association.

Simmerman, Steven. General Counsel, National Automobile Dealers Association.

Wagner, Paul. Executive Staff, United Automobile Workers.

Yingling, Jack. Executive Director, Support Group for Progressive Banking.

Anonymous. Member of the staff of the Proprietary Association.

Anonymous. Staff member of Office of the Federal Administrative Counsel, American Bankers Association.

Anonymous. Staff member of National Association of Manufacturers.

INTERVIEWS: NON-ORGANIZATION PERSONNEL

(All interviews took place in Washington, D.C.,
between June 5 and September 14, 1965.)

Clark, Senator Joseph S. Democrat, Pennsylvania.

Douglas, Senator Paul H. Democrat, Illinois.

Dym, Herbert. Attorney, Covington-Burling Law Firm.

Flynn, Clyde. Minority Counsel, Subcommittee on Constitutional Amendments, Senate Committee on the Judiciary.

Olson, Dr. T. K. Administrative Assistant to Senator Maurine Neuberger (Democrat, Oregon).

Pertschuk, Michael. General Counsel and Staff Member. Senate Commerce Committee.

Tupper, Ernest. Director, Tupper Associates, Washington, D.C.

Wolfe, Singleton. Executive Assistant to the Assistant Commissioner, Compliance Division, Internal Revenue Service, Washington, D.C.

Anonymous. Staff member of Senate Banking and Currency Committee.

SPEECHES AND UNPUBLISHED MATERIAL

May, Representative Catherine. Republican, Washington. "The Housewife Goes to Congress." 57th Annual Convention of the National Canners Association, Dallas, Texas, February 3, 1964.

Patman, Representative Wright. Democrat, Texas. "Remarks of the Honorable Wright Patman, Representative, First District of Texas to 22nd Annual Meeting of the National League of Insured Savings Associations, Beverly Hilton Hotel, Los Angeles, California," October 25, 1965.

Roberts, Clyde. "Marketing's Battle in Washington," given to unidentified business group, Washington, D.C., February, 1964.